INTERMITTENT FASTING FOR SMART WOMEN OVER 50

Easy Steps To Burn Fat and Lose Weight, Increase Energy and Regulate Metabolism With a 28-Day Eating Plan +155 Recipes (90 inside +65 downloadable)

SCAN THE QRCODE TO DOWNLOAD THE FREE BONUSES

OTHERWISE TYPE IN THIS ADDRESS:
https://bit.ly/3Q1U2yo

Annie Kerouak

© Copyright 2024 - *Annie Kerouak* - All rights reserved.

This document is geared towards providing exact and reliable information regarding the topic and issue covered. The publication is sold because the publisher is not required to render accounting, officially permitted, or otherwise qualified services. If advice is necessary, legal or professional, a practiced individual in the profession should be ordered.

- From a Declaration of Principles, which was accepted and approved equally by a Committee of the American Bar Association and a Committee of Publishers and Associations.

It is not legal to reproduce, duplicate, or transmit any part of this document electronically or in print. Recording this publication is strictly prohibited, and any storage of this document is not allowed unless with written permission from the publisher. All rights reserved.

The information provided herein is stated to be truthful and consistent. In terms of inattention or otherwise, any liability by any usage or abuse of any policies, processes, or directions contained within is the solitary and utter responsibility of the recipient reader. Under no circumstances will any legal responsibility or blame be held against the publisher for any reparation, damages, or monetary loss due to the information herein, either directly or indirectly.

Respective authors own all copyrights not held by the publisher.

The information herein is solely offered for informational purposes and is universal. The presentation of the information is without a contract or any guarantee assurance.

The trademarks used are without any consent, and the trademark publication is without permission or backing by the trademark owner. All trademarks and brands within this book are for clarifying purposes only and are owned by the owners, not affiliated with this document.

Table of Contents

Introduction 9
Section 1: The Science Behind Intermittent Fasting For Smart Women Over 50 14
Section 2: It's Just a Matter of MINDSET 28
Section 3: Weight Loss Psychology 35
Section 4: History and Principles 49
Section 5: Frequent Asked Questions & Answers 59
Section 6: Zero Deprivation Intermittent Fasting Tips 62
Section 7: 28-Day Meal Plan for the Busy Woman 66
Section 8: Conclusions 75
Section 9: Tasty Recipes 80

Tasty Breakfast Recipes 80

1. Avocado and Spinach Omelette 80
2. Greek Yogurt Parfait 81
3. Quinoa Breakfast Bowl 81
4. Smoked Salmon and Avocado Toast 82
5. Chia Seed Pudding 83
6. Veggie Frittata 84
7. Blueberry Almond Smoothie 84
8. Cottage Cheese with Pineapple 85
9. Banana Nut Overnight Oats 85
10. Spinach and Mushroom Breakfast Wrap 86
11. Apple Cinnamon Quinoa Porridge 87
12. Peanut Butter Banana Smoothie 88

13.	Berry Protein Pancakes	88
14.	Mediterranean Egg Muffins	89
15.	Tropical Green Smoothie Bowl	90

Satisfying Lunch Recipes 92

16.	Avocado and Chickpea Salad	92
17.	Quinoa and Roasted Vegetable Bowl	92
18.	Greek Salad with Grilled Chicken	93
19.	Salmon and Asparagus Foil Packets	94
20.	Turkey and Vegetable Stir-Fry	95
21.	Tofu and Veggie Lettuce Wraps	97
22.	Cauliflower Fried Rice	98
23.	Caprese Zucchini Noodles	99
24.	Lentil and Vegetable Soup	100
25.	Shrimp and Mango Salad	101
26.	Eggplant and Tomato Stacks	102
27.	Chicken and Spinach Salad with Raspberry Vinaigrette	103
28.	Tuna and White Bean Salad	104
29.	Ratatouille with Quinoa	104
30.	Baked Stuffed Bell Peppers	106

Nutrient-Dense Dinners: 107

31.	Salmon Avocado Salad	107
32.	Quinoa Stuffed Bell Peppers	108

33. Grilled Lemon Herb Chicken 109
34. Shrimp and Vegetable Stir-Fry 110
35. Turkey and Spinach Stuffed Portobello Mushrooms 111
36. Lentil and Vegetable Soup 112
37. Baked Cod with Lemon Herb Sauce 113
38. Veggie and Tofu Stir-Fry 114
39. Eggplant Parmesan 115
40. Chicken and Vegetable Skewers 116
41. Butternut Squash and Kale Salad 117
42. Beef and Broccoli Stir-Fry 118
43. Mediterranean Chickpea Salad 119
44. Cauliflower Rice Stir-Fry 120
45. Greek Yogurt Chicken Salad 121

Snacks 122

46. Avocado and Tomato Salad 122
47. Greek Yogurt with Berries 123
48. Cucumber Hummus Bites 123
49. Almond Butter and Banana Rice Cakes 124
50. Caprese Skewers 124
51. Smoked Salmon and Cucumber Rolls 125
52. Egg Salad Lettuce Wraps 126
53. Zucchini Chips 126

54. Tuna Stuffed Mini Bell Peppers 127
55. Cottage Cheese with Pineapple 128
56. Walnut and Apple Slices 128
57. Tofu and Vegetable Skewers 129
58. Quinoa Salad with Chickpeas 130
59. Roasted Chickpeas 131
60. Chocolate Covered Strawberries 131

Hydration and Beverages 132

61. Lemon Cucumber Mint Infused Water 132
62. Pineapple Ginger Green Tea 133
63. Watermelon Lime Electrolyte Drink 134
64. Berry Blast Hydration Smoothie 134
65. Citrus Mint Cooler 135
66. Cucumber Basil Detox Water 136
67. Mango Coconut Water Refresher 137
68. Raspberry Rosemary Infused Water 137
69. Turmeric Ginger Lemonade 138
70. Blueberry Basil Smash 139
71. Peach Lavender Iced Tea 140
72. Apple Cinnamon Spice Infused Water 141
73. Pomegranate Mint Spritzer 141
74. Watermelon Basil Cooler 142

75.	Kiwi Mint Refresher	143
	Dessert:	144
76.	Avocado Chocolate Mousse	144
77.	Greek Yogurt Parfait	144
78.	Banana Nice Cream	145
79.	Chia Seed Pudding	146
80.	Apple Slices with Almond Butter	146
81.	Coconut Yogurt with Mixed Berries	147
82.	Chocolate Covered Strawberries	147
83.	Mango Coconut Chia Pudding	148
84.	Nutty Date Balls	149
85.	Grilled Pineapple with Cinnamon	150
86.	Raspberry Coconut Chia Popsicles	150
87.	Almond Flour Cookies	151
88.	Lemon Blueberry Frozen Yogurt	152
89.	Peanut Butter Banana Bites	153
90.	Watermelon Mint Salad	153

FREE SUPPLEMENTARY STUDY RESOURCES 155

FREE SUPPLEMENTARY STUDY RESOURCES

√ 65 Flash Cards with additional special recipes for your intermittent fasting.

√ 28-Day Food Plan printable board to hang in your kitchen

SCAN THE QRCODE TO DOWNLOAD THE FREE BONUSES

OTHERWISE TYPE IN THIS ADDRESS:

https://bit.ly/3Q1U2yo

Improve your awareness of how to burn superfluous fat and lose weight by boosting your energy and regulating your metabolism with our exclusive free bonus, included in the book "INTERMITTENT FASTING FOR SMART WOMEN OVER 50."

Expand your results with our free downloadable resources by experts. These tools, designed to enhance your knowledge and refine your approach to intermittent fasting, are the key to unlocking the next level of success.

Introduction

Clara gazes intently at the brightly colored packages of vitamins and medications lined up before her on the kitchen table. It has become a matter of utmost importance.

Weight gain. Decreased energy. Laziness. Depression.

The scale, seemingly inconspicuous in the corner, had become the supreme judge, along with the mirror, of the drama Clara experiences daily, firsthand. That same mirror that, until a few years ago, reflected a pleasing image of herself. Now, Clara no longer recognizes or likes what she sees.

She had pinned her hopes and desires on each of those colorful boxes. The latest purchase, those "energizing" pills that promised to suppress her appetite, only served to deepen her depression.

Each colorful package claimed to be the elixir, the miraculous remedy, the cure-all for her condition of being "differently slim." But, despite all her resolutions and diligent attempts to stick to diet and fitness programs, the numbers on the scale continue to climb while her energy diminishes with each passing day.

Do you personally know someone like Clara?

She is just one of many people stuck in a frustrating loop of failed diets and depression. There are many like her in this situation.

As we age, it becomes increasingly difficult to maintain a suitable weight and a lifestyle aligned with the performance that modern society demands, especially for people, and women in particular, who are over 50.

But what if I told you there exists a system, a path that doesn't require limiting your diet, engaging in strenuous gym sessions, or stocking your medicine cabinet with a range of expensive supplements?

What would you think?

For a brief moment, imagine that the key to unlocking your body's full potential lies not in a technique, but in a very simple and highly effective concept. Our ancestors knew it, but it was long ignored.

This key can become your guide to regain control of your health, reignite your vitality, and achieve your weight loss and mental well-being goals, without giving up the joy of food or the ability to enjoy life on your terms.

"Intermittent Fasting For Smart Women Over 50" is your guide to achieving all these goals.

If you want, my friend (perhaps over 50), you can take advantage of this opportunity, and enter with mind and heart into the vast resource that this book represents.

I wish to extend a warm welcome to you as you are about to discover the transformative power of Intermittent Fasting. A method that, as has been scientifically proven, will not only help you shed those excess pounds but will also enhance your health and overall well-being in ways you never thought possible.

"Intermittent fasting enhances health, overall well-being, and boosts energy. Only as a direct consequence does it lead to weight loss. What could be better than such a significant side effect?"

In the pages that follow, you will discover its great power.

However, before we delve into the mechanics of how intermittent fasting can radically revolutionize your life, let's take a moment to acknowledge the challenges you might be facing right now. You may have tried various diets in the past, only to find yourself back at your original weight or, even worse, heavier than before you started.

You might be struggling with these issues: low energy levels, chronic cravings, a sense of frustration and defeat that seems to overshadow every attempt at self-improvement. If you suffer from even one of these symptoms, it's important to remember that you are not alone and that there is hope for a healthier, better future.

Take the time to read this book. Compared to the plethora of other diet and fitness books vying for your attention, what sets "Intermittent Fasting For Smart Women Over 50" apart from the rest?

The answer can be found in the unique method provided here. It's a strategy tailored to the needs and challenges of people over the age of 40/50 who are looking for sustainable, long-term solutions to their health and weight loss goals.

This system is based on scientific principles and supported by decades of research, unlike many trendy diets that promise immediate results and quick fixes.

When practicing intermittent fasting, you're able to leverage the body's existing fat-burning mechanisms, boost metabolism, and access a multitude of health benefits that extend far beyond weight reduction. To achieve this, you must first learn to harness your body's natural rhythms and align your eating patterns with the innate wisdom of your organism.

Reading this book will allow you to understand how intermittent fasting can help you break free from the yo-yo dieting cycle and achieve lasting results, sustainable throughout your life. As you progress through the book, you will learn how this simple yet effective practice can not only help you shed those stubborn pounds but also enhance your cognitive functions, increase your energy levels, and reduce the likelihood of developing chronic diseases such as diabetes, heart disease, and Alzheimer's, to name a few. In addition to regaining your vitality and well-being, you can achieve all this while enjoying nutritious, delicious, and satisfying meals.

However, the most important discovery you will make is that intermittent fasting is not just another diet, but rather a lifestyle. This is perhaps the most crucial lesson you will learn. Regardless of your age or the stage of life you are in, it is about adopting a new way of eating that not only nourishes your body, mind, and soul but also offers you the opportunity to live your life to the fullest.

This holds true regardless of your physical constitution. Moreover, you will have a trusted guide by your side throughout this journey of self-discovery. This will be true at every stage of the adventure.

As an author, the work of my life, which also includes creating this book, is dedicated to supporting women and people, not yet fully aware, in realizing their full potential and achieving the highest possible level of health and fitness.

I personally practice Intermittent Fasting as a system to enhance my physical and mental well-being. Once you have learned and mastered the system, you can use it as needed, just as I do. Therefore, I truly hope that my testimony and my book will be useful to you. Over my many years of experience in the field of nutrition, fitness, and holistic health, I have had the opportunity to personally observe the enormous impact that intermittent fasting can have on improving lives, including my own. Now, I am excited to share with you my experience, insights, and proven methods, so that you too can experience the benefits of intermittent fasting. And embark on a journey towards a happier, healthier, and more aware version of yourself.

Therefore, I invite you to discover the transformative power of intermittent fasting.

Be ready to say goodbye to the endless cycle of diets and disappointments and welcome a future full of energy, vitality, and joy that will change your life and promise a radiant future. With the pounds you want to lose, of course.

Section 1: The Science Behind Intermittent Fasting For Smart Women Over 50

Unlocking the Power of Intermittent Fasting

Intermittent fasting, which is a specific dietary strategy that alternates between times of eating and fasting, has caught a lot of attention recently due to the possible health benefits it may offer, particularly for women who are over the age of 50. In this chapter, we will cover the benefits of intermittent fasting for women in this age range, as well as the reasoning for its scientific foundation.

Understanding Intermittent Fasting

In the practice of intermittent fasting, the window of opportunity, or the amount of time during which a person is able to ingest food, is minimized to the greatest extent possible. The 16/8 method, which entails fasting for sixteen hours and eating within an eight-hour window, and the 5:2 method, which entails taking fewer calories for two days that are not consecutive each week, are two additional approaches that can be utilized to accomplish this goal. It is possible that the practice of intermittent fasting will result in weight loss because it reduces the overall amount of calories consumed every day. One method for accomplishing this is to cut down on the amount of time that is available for eating.

Metabolic Benefits

Intermittent fasting has many metabolic benefits, in addition to its ability to help people lose weight. One of the most important factors that contribute to its effectiveness is the influence that it has on insulin sensitivity. This causes insulin levels to decline, which in turn causes the body to consume glucose that has been stored as a source of energy. This can, over time, lead to better insulin sensitivity, which in turn reduces the chance of developing metabolic syndrome and type 2 diabetes, both of which are conditions that, as people get older, become more widespread.

Cellular Repair and Longevity

Autophagy, a process in which cells remove defective components and recycle them for energy, is one of the cellular repair processes that can be triggered by intermittent fasting. The body gets cleansed on a cellular level through this procedure, which may also contribute to the body's ability to live longer. Additionally, it has been demonstrated that intermittent fasting can increase the synthesis of neurotrophic factors, which are beneficial to the health of the brain and cognitive function, as well as upregulate genes that are connected with greater longevity.

Hormonal Balance

When it comes to weight management and overall health, women over the age of 50 may face special obstacles as a result of the hormonal changes that are linked with menopause. The practice of intermittent fasting has been discovered to have an effect on hormone levels in ways that may be especially advantageous for this particular population sector. By way of illustration, it may result in an increase in the synthesis of growth hormone, which is involved in the process of fat metabolism and the maintenance of muscle mass. In addition, intermittent fasting may be able to assist in the regulation of estrogen levels, which in turn may lessen the likelihood of developing tumors related to hormones and alleviate the symptoms of menopause.

Inflammation Reduction

A wide variety of age-related ailments, including Alzheimer's disease, arthritis, and heart disease, have been linked to chronic inflammation, which is a trait that is usually associated with the aging process. Chronic inflammation has also been linked to several other age-related conditions. Interleukin-6 and C-reactive protein are two examples of inflammatory indicators that have been shown to be lowered in the body through the practice of intermittent fasting. This has been demonstrated through scientific experimentation. There is a possibility that engaging in the practice of intermittent fasting will lessen the likelihood of experiencing a variety of ailments, as well as improve overall health and vitality. The reduction of the inflammatory response facilitates the achievement of this goal.

Brain Health and Cognitive Function

Many women are concerned that as they become older, they will experience a reduction in their cognitive abilities.

However, there is some evidence that suggests that intermittent fasting may provide protection against age-related cognitive decline as well as several neurodegenerative diseases. Synaptic plasticity, memory function, and the production of brain-derived neurotrophic factor (BDNF), a protein that enables neurons to grow and survive, have all been found to be improved with the practice of intermittent fasting. The research that was carried out on animals has demonstrated that these characteristics are beneficial. According to these findings, it would indicate that intermittent fasting may have neuroprotective effects and may be able to assist in the preservation of cognitive function well beyond the point at which one retires early.

Practical Considerations

It is vital that the practice of intermittent fasting be undertaken with caution, particularly for women who are over the age of 50, despite the fact that the scientific data that supports it is overwhelming. When commencing a program of intermittent fasting, it is strongly suggested that you seek the guidance of a trained medical professional before beginning the program. This is of utmost significance for persons who are coping with previous health difficulties or who are utilizing drugs that have the potential to adversely affect their ability to fast. Additionally, it is crucial to pay attention to your body and make any necessary adjustments to your fasting routine in order to guarantee that it is in accordance with your particular requirements and way of life. This is the only way to ensure that your fasting routine is effective.

There is a possibility that the dietary strategy of intermittent fasting could be beneficial for women over the age of 50 who are clever and who are attempting to improve their health and well-being. By taking advantage of the metabolic, hormonal, and cellular benefits that fasting offers, women in this age range can support weight control, promote longevity, and protect themselves against age-related disorders. Furthermore, they can protect themselves against age-related disorders. If it is approached with careful consideration and supervision, intermittent fasting has the potential to be a very helpful tool in the pursuit of optimal health and vigor in the second half of life. However, caution and monitoring are required in order to achieve this goal.

A significant number of people all around the world are confronted with an ongoing challenge of losing weight. There is a plethora of fad diets, wonder medications, and quick-fix remedies that promise to cut the time it takes to achieve the ideal body with shortcuts. On the other hand, the unpleasant reality is that the majority of these strategies do not produce benefits that are sustainable over time. In spite of the wealth of information that is currently available, the prevalence of obesity continues to increase, which demonstrates that traditional methods of weight loss are insufficient.

Through this discussion, we will investigate the shortcomings of conventional weight-loss diets and advocate for a paradigm shift toward reasoned intermittent fasting as a viable alternative to typical diets. It is possible for individuals to adopt better habits without falling into the vicious cycle of dieting and deprivation if they have a sufficient awareness of the ideas that underlie this approach and the potential benefits that it may offer.

The Fallacy of Weight-Loss Diets

The attractiveness of weight-loss regimens lies in the fact that they promise low work and speedy results in a short amount of time. There are a variety of diet plans available on the market, ranging from paleo to keto, low-carb to low-fat, and everything in between. Each of these diet plans claims to be the best way to get rid of excess weight. On the other hand, the reality is far different from what these diets claim to be.

Conventional weight loss plans are characterized by their emphasis on restriction and deprivation, which is one of the most fundamental problems in these diets. A negative connection with food is created by these diets, which are characterized by the demonization of specific food groups or the imposition of stringent calorie limits. This results in feelings of shame and failure when the inevitable slip-ups occur. Furthermore, the restricted nature of these diets frequently results in food deficits, a reduction in metabolic rate, and even instances of binge eating, which ultimately undermines efforts to lose weight over the long run.

Additionally, the majority of diets that are designed to help people lose weight do not address the fundamental issues that contribute to weight gain. These variables include hormone imbalances, emotional eating, and lifestyle choices. They instead provide a one-size-fits-all strategy that ignores individual differences and preferences, which makes it difficult to stick to the guidelines and ensures that they cannot be maintained over the long term.

Reasoned Intermittent Fasting: A Paradigm Shift

Reasoned intermittent fasting provides a novel approach to obtaining and sustaining a healthy weight, in contrast to the conventional weight-loss programs that are commonly used. Rather than concentrating exclusively on the foods that should be consumed, this strategy places an emphasis on the timing of meals, thereby utilizing the inherent processes that the body possesses to facilitate fat reduction and metabolic wellness.

Reasoned intermittent fasting is based on the fundamental premise of alternating periods of eating and fasting. This enables the body to enter a state known as ketosis, which is defined by the body using its fat stores as a source of energy. Reasoned intermittent fasting is simpler to incorporate into daily life since it adopts a more adaptable and durable strategy. This is not the case with typical fasting methods, which require prolonged periods of not eating or drinking.

The key principles of reasoned intermittent fasting include:

1. Flexible Fasting Windows: Reasoned intermittent fasting, in contrast to rigorous fasting regimes, enables individuals to personalize their fasting windows in

accordance with their lifestyle and preferences. No matter if you choose to fast for 16 hours, 18 hours, or alternate days, the objective is to achieve a calorie deficit without experiencing feelings of deprivation or hunger.

2. Contrary to what most people believe, intermittent fasting is not about starvation but rather about strategically timing meals. This is because nutrient-rich fasting is a method of eating. Individuals are urged to consume nutrient-dense foods that are beneficial to their general health and well-being during feasting periods. Individuals are able to nourish their bodies while still accomplishing their weight loss goals if they place a higher priority on quality than quantity consumption.

3. Consumption with Mindfulness: Intermittent fasting encourages mindfulness with regard to the selection of foods and the routines of eating. It is possible for individuals to cultivate a more positive relationship with food and steer clear of mindless eating patterns that contribute to weight gain if they become more receptive to the signals that indicate when they are hungry and when they are full.

4. Metabolic Flexibility: The body is trained to become more metabolically flexible via the practice of fasting, which enables it to switch between burning glucose and fat for fuel in a more efficient manner. The reduction of inflammation, improvement of insulin sensitivity, and

enhancement of metabolic health are all outcomes that result from this. In addition, fat loss is facilitated.

The Feast: Finding Balance and Enjoyment

It is be that the concept of the feast is the component of reasoned intermittent fasting that appears to be the most tempting. The practice of intermittent fasting encourages individuals to appreciate the pleasure of food without feeling guilty or restricting themselves in any way, in contrast to typical diets that stigmatize particular foods and create a rigid "good versus bad" worldview.

During the feast, which is a celebration of food and the pleasure of eating, there are no foods that are not permitted to be consumed. Individuals are encouraged to savor the flavors, textures, and scents of their favorite dishes, which helps to promote a sense of contentment and fulfillment. This is in contrast to the traditional view of meals as only a means to an end.

On the other hand, the feast is not at all a mindless and unrestrained binge fest; rather, it is a conscious and deliberate indulgence. Individuals are able to indulge in their preferred foods without jeopardizing their progress or jeopardizing their health if they adhere to the concepts of moderation and balance. This strategy not only enables individuals to adhere to their diets more closely, but it also improves their general pleasure and sense of well-being.

The Cycle of Reasoned Intermittent Fasting

It is the cyclical character of reasoned intermittent fasting that is the most important factor in its success. Instead of considering fasting as a short-term solution, individuals are urged to accept it as a lifestyle habit that may be maintained over time. Typically, the cycle consists of alternating between times of fasting and feasting. This allows the body to adjust to the new circumstances and improve the efficiency of its metabolic processes over time.

In the course of fasting, the body goes through a number of physiological changes that are beneficial to the reduction of fat and the repair of damaged cells. For instance, autophagy is a cellular cleansing process that takes place while fasting. It assists in the removal of damaged cells and contributes to an overall improvement in human health. A further benefit of fasting is that it has been demonstrated to raise levels of growth hormone, which is an essential component in the process of fat metabolism and the maintenance of muscle mass.

Feasting, on the other hand, offers the chance to refuel one's energy reserves and to take pleasure in the experience. It is possible for individuals to boost the growth of their muscles, replace their glycogen stores, and improve their recovery from fasting periods by providing their bodies with nutrient-rich foods. Additionally, feasting helps to preserve metabolic flexibility and prevents metabolic adaption, which ensures that progress is made toward weight loss objectives despite the fact that feasting is occurring.

Not only is the cycle of reasoned intermittent fasting good for weight loss, but it also enhances overall health and longevity. There are several benefits associated with this cycle. The practice of intermittent fasting is in line with our evolutionary biology and metabolic physiology since it involves imitating the eating patterns of our ancestors, who went through times of both feasting and starvation. As a consequence of this, it provides a method of health and well-being that is more sustainable and holistic.

Overcoming Challenges and Building Resilience

Even while there are a lot of potential advantages to be gained via reasoned intermittent fasting, it is not without its difficulties. As the body changes to new eating patterns and metabolic processes, an adaptation to fasting may require some time and patience on the part of the individual. Fasting can be challenging for a number of reasons, including the social influences and cultural conventions that surround eating, particularly in a country where food is frequently associated with socialization and celebration.

On the other hand, individuals are able to successfully overcome these challenges and develop resilience on their road toward improved health if they are provided with the appropriate information, support, and guidance. It is possible to reduce cravings and increase adherence to fasting protocols by employing techniques such as meal planning, mindful eating, and stress management. In addition, establishing connections with people who have similar values and seeking help from specialists in the healthcare field may be extremely beneficial in terms of providing encouragement and accountability.

In conclusion, the prevalent narrative around weight loss programs has to be questioned because they frequently fail to offer outcomes that are sustainable and prolong a cycle of deprivation and disappointment. A feasible alternative that makes use of the natural mechanisms of the body to improve fat reduction, metabolic health, and overall well-being is the practice of intermittent fasting, which is based on rational explanations.

By adopting intermittent fasting as a lifestyle practice rather than a short-term solution, individuals are able to obtain long-term outcomes without compromising their happiness or sense of fulfillment. Because the cycle of fasting and feasting is in harmony with our evolutionary biology and metabolic physiology, it is a method that is both practical and efficient for managing weight over the long term.

As we continue to negotiate the complexity of modern life, let us reclaim our relationship with food and embrace a more balanced and sustainable approach to health and wellbeing. This will help us to better support ourselves and our families. Developing resiliency, empowering ourselves with information, and embarking on a journey toward a life that is healthier, happier, and more meaningful are all possible outcomes that can be achieved via the practice of moderate intermittent fasting.

Managing Menopause Symptoms through Intermittent Fasting:

- Research indicates that there is a potential benefit to intermittent fasting in reducing some of the common menopausal symptoms, such as hot flashes and night sweats.

- In addition to bringing about a stabilization of blood sugar levels and a reduction in inflammation, intermittent fasting has the potential to improve mood and energy levels during this period of transition.

- Incorporating intermittent fasting into a menopausal woman's lifestyle can be accomplished through the use of practical techniques, such as progressively increasing the length of fasting intervals and maintaining proper hydration levels during fasting hours.

Balancing Hormones for Overall Well-being:

- For general health and wellbeing, a balanced hormonal balance is crucial; this is particularly true for women over 50 going through menopause.

- Intermittent fasting has the potential to assist in the regulation of many hormones, including insulin, cortisol, and growth hormone, all of which play important roles in the metabolism, the response to stress, and the repair of cells.

- In this study, we look into the possible long-term health benefits of intermittent fasting for women as well as how it can support the maintenance of hormonal homeostasis.

Addressing Hormonal Fluctuations with Dietary Strategies:

- Additionally, certain dietary practices can further improve hormonal balance during menopause. These methods can be used in conjunction with intermittent fasting.

- It is possible to enhance hormone production and regulation by placing an emphasis on nutrient-dense foods that are rich in vital vitamins and minerals. Some examples of such foods include almonds, fatty fish, and leafy greens.

- There are certain foods that are known for their ability to balance hormones, such as flaxseeds, soy products, and cruciferous vegetables. These foods should be incorporated into meals and snacks regularly.

- During menopause, it is important to prioritize hormone-balancing foods and maintain general health. This can be accomplished through functional meal ideas and recipes.

Section 2: It's Just a Matter of MINDSET

Believe it or not, to achieve any goal in life, 90% is about mindset, your mental attitude, while the remaining 10% is about technique, which includes knowledge and actions.

Some might fall off their chairs reading this statement. Others might start calculating probabilities in their minds, assigning percentages that better suit their personal beliefs, both conscious and subconscious (paradigms). For example, "yes, attitude is important, but in my opinion, it's 20% mindset and 80% technique. Others might think it's 50/50, half and half.

Dear readers, the point here isn't to nail the exact percentage or to take my word for it. It's the science of Personal Growth that has established these numerical factors with precise statistical criteria. The important thing is for you to understand how crucial, how truly significant, your mental attitude towards your goals and especially towards yourselves, or rather the image you have of yourselves, is.

"But what about Usain Bolt, Enzo Maiorca, Messi, three 'sacred deities' of the sports world, who have set Guinness World Records, then? You surely can't make me believe that for them, too, what mattered most in achieving their world records was 90% mindset and only 10% technique? They trained exhaustively for a lifetime!" Some readers might argue something like this.

- Usain Bolt, the sprinter, shattered every previous record in 2009 by running 100 meters in 9.58 seconds, averaging almost 38 km/h.
- Enzo Maiorca, the king of free-diving, reached a depth of 101 meters in 1988 on a single breath, diving into the sea and setting what was then a world record.
- Lionel Messi, "La Pulce" (The Flea) nicknamed for his short stature, suffered from a mild form of dwarfism as a child. He has been declared the world's best football player by FIFA and UEFA, winning multiple Ballon d'Or and Golden Shoe awards. He is also a UNICEF ambassador and founder of the Lionel Messi Foundation, which helps underprivileged children with health problems.

These three sporting legends are just an example drawn deliberately from the sports universe. It would have been too easy to use genius figures like Leonardo da Vinci, Marie Curie, Albert Einstein, Rita Levi Montalcini to exemplify the 90% mindset, 10% technique theory.

Bolt, Maiorca, Messi, had to work hard in training their bodies, no doubt. But what they did and continue to do every day, some more, some less, like all athletes around the world, is their winning card. It was believing, having faith, and unconditional trust in the image they had of themselves. In their minds, they already saw themselves as winners. They experienced, before achieving them, the emotions and sensations their records would bring them. They never doubted that they might not make it. And even if, humanly, this thought occurred to them, they replaced it with the beauty of the sensations of victory they would feel.

Am I advising you to deceive your mind, while you imagine proudly showing off your swimsuit body? Labels stuck onto your goals only serve to prevent you from reaching them if they are contrary to the goal. But if they are favorable and help achieve it, why not?

After all, isn't your mind deceiving you when it tells you that you'll never be in perfect shape for the swimsuit season? Do what is useful for you and your goals, and don't pay attention to the judgments of your inner voice; it acts this way because of years of old beliefs rooted in your habits. The solution is to install small new habits in your daily life that are favorable and help you achieve your goals.

Small New Habits That Will Change Your Life:

- When you go to the supermarket, avoid putting junk food in your cart. Only buy high-nutritional quality foods, checking off the list you wrote at home.

- If you have established your intermittent fasting plan, such as the 16/8 which involves skipping breakfast, prepare a long, unsweetened tea or coffee.

- While sipping your coffee, reread the pages of this chapter on mindset, which will help you stay focused on your goals and remind you why you are doing it.

- Find a photo of yourself when you liked how you looked or an online image of someone else that represents and reflects you without the need for supermodels or actors with unattainable physical features. A girl/boy-next-door type with whom you resonate will do. Print several copies: one to stick on the refrigerator, one on the headboard of your bed, one on the bathroom mirror, and save one as the wallpaper on your smartphone and computer.

- Avoid television programs about recipes and restaurant challenges.

- Join social groups that support the intermittent fasting journey you have embarked on and turn on notifications. Reading and interacting with people who have been in your shoes at the beginning will be of great help and support. As you progress, you will find yourself supporting other newcomers, and only then will you understand the benefits you derive. For now, you just have to trust and sign up.

- Write a gratitude list, a list of things you are grateful for. Whether on paper or typed in the notes on your smartphone, pull it out and read it every time you have negative thoughts or think you can't make it. If the list of things you are grateful for in life is sincere, when you read it, item by item, connect to the emotions deriving from it and let yourself be overwhelmed by them. For example, I am grateful for: my son/daughter. Think of the most beautiful moments lived with them: the first time they latched to your breast, the first word they spoke, when they first stood up on their wobbly legs, when you first let them pedal alone on their shiny bike, the first day of school, graduation, the first date, the day of their thesis defense, when they made you grandparents... Connect with these emotions, let yourself be overwhelmed, live them, visualize them.

- By the end of your list, all the negativity that gripped your mind and stomach will be pulverized and gone. Your vibrations will be sky-high, and the frequencies of your positive thoughts will attract other positive thoughts, giving you confidence and esteem in yourself and the world around you, making you a slightly better person each time you do it.

- Take time to carefully prepare the meals that belong to you during the 8 hours of feeding in your 16/8 program. Smell the ingredients of the recipes, you will discover that a bell pepper, a slice of salmon, or a lemon are no longer the same as before the program. They will have a fuller aroma, a rounder flavor, a note unknown to you. Increase your awareness, this is the path to follow. At the beginning, you may not see its utility, but in the short term, just a few days, and you will start to see an increase in energy. And after just a couple of weeks, the benefits will be evident to your eyes and to the decreasing numbers on your scale.

- After a month or two, you will likely become volunteer ambassadors of intermittent fasting, if it suits you, do it.

Suddenly everyone will notice your energetic changes and attitude towards everyday life situations and will ask you for explanations and advice. If you like, do it, with the modesty of the apprentice, but do it.

- Talk about yourself and your results. There is no need to enter into medical and health contexts that are not your expertise. It is enough to talk about your 90% mental approach, because everything starts from there, and the technical program, the remaining 10%: 16-hour intervals and 8 hours of feeding with high-nutrient foods, with the recipes you will find in the following pages.
- Cultivate patience with activities and hobbies useful for its growth. You will benefit during meal waiting times and, in cascade, in every sector of your life.

On the other hand, motivated individuals are able to successfully overcome any challenge and develop resilience on their journey towards better health if they receive the right information, support, and guidance. With a few small new habits, it is possible to reduce cravings and increase adherence to fasting protocols using techniques such as meal planning, mindful eating, and stress management. Moreover, forming connections with people who have similar goals and values and seeking help from healthcare professionals can be extremely helpful in terms of encouragement and accountability. In conclusion, the prevailing narrative around all diet programs for weight loss must be questioned, as they often do not offer sustainable results in the medium and long term and prolong a cycle of deprivation and disappointment. A feasible alternative that leverages the body's natural mechanisms to improve fat reduction, metabolic health, and overall well-being is the practice of intermittent fasting, which is based on rational, scientific, and anthropological explanations. By adopting intermittent fasting as a lifestyle rather than a short-term solution, individuals are able to achieve long-term results without compromising their happiness or sense of fulfillment. Since the cycle of fasting and feeding is in harmony with our evolutionary biology and metabolic physiology, it is a practical and effective method for managing weight in the long term. Isn't this what each of us would want: to manage weight and well-being in the long term? As we continue to navigate the complexities of modern life, let's reclaim our relationship with food and embrace a more balanced and sustainable approach to health and wellness. This will help us better support ourselves and our families. Developing resilience, gaining knowledge, and embarking on a journey towards a healthier, happier, and more meaningful life are all possible outcomes that can be achieved with the practice of intermittent fasting.

Section 3: Weight Loss Psychology

Psychologically, more often than not, it is the meaning we each assign to the word "fasting" that instills fear in us. False beliefs, war and famine stories narrated by our grandparents and great-grandparents, movies and books about deportation and concentration camps... All these have contributed to creating beliefs and paradigms in our subconscious that invisibly guide us through life.

Let's try calling it **"scheduled food abstinence"** instead of intermittent fasting. Hear how that sounds better? Notice how the fear disappears?

In their efforts to reduce body fat percentage, many people embark on a journey that includes various diets, exercise routines, and lifestyle changes. However, the power of mindset, or mental attitude, is sometimes overlooked despite the abundance of ideas and techniques available. Losing weight is not just a physical challenge but a mental one too. In the previous chapter, we discussed how the right mindset can act as a catalyst to achieve weight loss goals, transforming dissatisfaction into determination and unleashing the latent superpowers within us.

Understanding the Mental Component of Weight Loss

Before delving into the complex psychology of human behavior and its role in weight loss, it's essential to have a solid understanding of the mental aspect of the process. Losing weight is not just about shedding pounds, but rather changing habits, beliefs, and perceptions to achieve the desired results. Many people struggle not because they are incapable of performing the tasks required, but because they believe they do not possess the mental strength to carry out these actions regularly.

The Psychology of Weight Loss

There are many cognitive and emotional factors to consider when discussing the psychology of weight loss. Individuals often face internal blocks that prevent them from progressing. These challenges can be rooted habits or issues with self-image. Developing strategies to overcome these psychological complexities and fostering the right mindset for success requires a deep understanding of these approaches.

Self-Perception and Body Image

Improving self-perception and body image is a crucial component of the psychology of weight loss. The way people view themselves greatly impacts their motivation levels and confidence, as well as their overall attitude towards losing weight. A positive self-perception can empower individuals to take control of their health and well-being, while a negative self-view can fuel self-doubt and undermine efforts to improve an individual's health and wellness.

The Power of Inner Dialogue

Inner dialogue, also known as the internal voice that people use to communicate with themselves, significantly influences their mindset and behavioral patterns. Negative self-talk can contribute to feelings of inadequacy and failure, while positive conversations can help promote resilience and perseverance. To establish a mindset conducive to successful weight loss, leveraging the power of inner dialogue is an essential component.

Goal Setting and Visualization

There are powerful strategies that can be used to shape mindset and behavior, such as:

- Setting clear and achievable goals
- Imagining their realization

Visualization stimulates the subconscious mind, which in turn strengthens the belief in being able to achieve set goals

Goals provide direction and purpose. To advance their weight loss journey, individuals can leverage the power of goal setting and visualization, aligning their mindset with the goals they wish to achieve.

Overcoming Self-Sabotage and Fear of Failure

There are many obstacles that can slow down the weight loss process, including self-sabotage and fear of failure. It is essential to overcome these internal barriers to cultivate a resilient attitude. These obstacles may include giving in to cravings, postponing physical exercise, or undermining progress for fear of success. People can overcome self-sabotage and embrace obstacles along the weight reduction path by viewing failure as an opportunity for growth and learning.

Building Resilience and Perseverance

Resilience and perseverance are two of the most important characteristics of a successful weight loss mindset. Inevitably, there will be obstacles and failures along the way; however, the way individuals react to these difficulties ultimately determines the level of success they achieve. Developing skills, seeking help when needed, and maintaining a positive outlook in the face of adversity are all vital components in cultivating resilience.

The Role of Social Support

During the weight loss process, the influence of social support on a person's mindset and behavior is crucial. It helps to have a support network that can provide encouragement, accountability, and practical help. This support network can consist of friends, family, or online communities. In times of difficulty, it can be beneficial to surround oneself with people who have similar goals and values. This can help strengthen positive habits and consolidate resilience.

Cultivating Mindfulness and Self-Compassion

A healthy mindset is necessary for weight loss, and two crucial components of this mindset are self-compassion and mindfulness. Being present in the moment and promoting awareness of one's thoughts and feelings without passing judgment on them are both components of mindfulness. A person who practices self-compassion is someone who treats themselves with love and understanding, especially in times of difficulty or when experiencing a setback. People can develop a more balanced and resilient approach to weight loss through the practice of mindfulness and self-compassion.

Leveraging the Power of Intermittent Fasting

Due to the potential benefits it can have for weight control, intermittent fasting—a dietary style that alternates periods of fasting and eating—has grown in popularity. Beyond physiological implications, intermittent fasting can impact an individual's mindset, promoting self-regulation, self-discipline, and a change in perspective towards food consumption. By using intermittent fasting as a tool for both physical and emotional transformation, people can harness its potential to accelerate their journey towards increased energy and weight loss.

When it comes to losing weight, thinking is often the missing piece of the puzzle. By recognizing mental barriers and challenges inherent in the journey, it is possible for anyone to harness the power of attitude to achieve their weight loss goals and embark on a path towards greater health, happiness, and energy. This can be achieved by cultivating self-awareness, resilience, and a positive outlook.

Eating Out and Socializing

Socializing and dining out are essential components of life as they offer the opportunity to reconnect with loved ones and friends and to experience a variety of cuisines. However, the act of dining out can be challenging for those trying to adhere to specific dietary goals or maintain a healthy lifestyle. It is possible to make healthy choices while still enjoying meals with your loved ones if you are willing to make some effort and gain some knowledge. Here are some tips for dining out and socializing without sacrificing your efforts to improve your health.

Alternatives to Unhealthy Restaurants

Dining out can feel like navigating a minefield of tempting but potentially unhealthy options, and choosing healthy items can be extremely challenging. However, if you keep some strategies in mind, you will be able to make choices that are beneficial for your health and well-being.

1. Research the Menu in Advance. Many restaurants now offer their menus online, allowing you to review the available options before arriving at the restaurant. Take advantage of this by scanning the menu for healthier

choices such as salads, grilled proteins, and vegetable-based dishes.
2. Consider Lean Protein Sources. When selecting a main dish, it is advisable to opt for lean protein sources such as grilled chicken, fish, or tofu, whenever possible. Compared to dishes with fried or breaded meats, these alternatives contain fewer calories and less saturated fat.
3. Vegetables Are a Good Choice for a well-balanced meal because they are rich in essential nutrients and fiber. Vegetables should be consumed in large quantities every day. Look for recipes that feature vegetables prominently, such as salads, stir-fries, or vegetable-based soups.
4. Watch Portion Sizes. People tend to overeat when dining out because portions are generally larger than what they would eat at home. To limit portions and avoid consuming an excessive amount of calories, consider ordering a half portion or sharing a dish with a dining companion.
5. Be Cautious with Sauces and Dressings. Many foods served in restaurants come with opulent sauces or dressings, which can add unnecessary calories and fats. If you want to control the amount of sauces and dressings you use, ask for them to be served on the side. Alternatively, you can ask for lighter options like vinaigrettes or salsa.
6. Dishes Rich in Added Sugars and Saturated Fats, such as fried appetizers, creamy sauces, and sweet cocktails,

should be avoided altogether. Limit your consumption of these foods. When it comes to supporting your dietary goals, choose healthier options whenever possible.

Social Events

The fact that social events often revolve around food and drinks makes it challenging to stick to dietary goals like intermittent fasting. However, there are smart strategies for participating in social gatherings. By adopting some clever methods, you can still manage social situations and enjoy time with friends and family.

1. Prepare in Advance: If you know you'll be attending a social event that involves eating, plan your eating schedule accordingly. Adjust your meal times or fasting window so you don't feel deprived while participating in the event.
2. Focus on Socializing, Not Just Food: Although food is often the focal point of social events, it's important to remember that the primary goal is to connect with others and enjoy each other's company during the event. Shift your focus from the food to the conversation and shared experiences.
3. Eat Mindfully: When you do partake in a meal at social gatherings, eat mindfully, savoring each bite slowly and paying attention to your body's hunger and fullness

signals. The best defense against mindless eating is to stay aware and engaged with your surroundings.
4. When presented with a buffet or a selection of appetizers, it is crucial to carefully examine the available options and choose items that align with your dietary goals. Increase your intake of vegetables, lean meats, and whole grains, while reducing consumption of less nutritious options like fried foods and sweets.
5. Whether dining out or attending social events, don't be afraid to be assertive about your choices. Your dietary preferences and goals should be communicated. It's important to politely decline foods that don't meet your dietary requirements and feel empowered to make decisions that benefit your health and well-being.
6. Staying Hydrated is Important: Drinking water throughout the event will help you feel full and satisfied, thus reducing the temptation to indulge in less nutritious options. Additionally, maintaining proper hydration is crucial for overall health and well-being.

By applying these tactics, you will be able to manage social situations and dining out while maintaining your commitment to health and dietary goals. Remember that moderation and awareness are key to success, and it's acceptable to indulge occasionally, as long as you do so mindfully. If you organize yourself in advance and pay attention to your surroundings, you can enjoy socializing and good food without derailing your progress toward a healthier lifestyle.

Mindful Eating Practices

Initially, in a society where people live at a hectic pace and are constantly distracted by other things, the act of eating has transformed into a mundane task rather than a purposeful experience. Mindful eating techniques, however, offer us the opportunity to reestablish a connection with our bodies, develop a deeper appreciation for food, and ultimately support the development of a healthy relationship with eating. This journey towards a more mindful attitude towards food is illuminated by two essential concepts of mindful eating:

- Savoring each bite slowly
- Listening to hunger signals These ideas serve as a guide.

Savoring Each Bite Slowly: The act of savoring each bite requires us to slow down and fully immerse ourselves in the sensory experience of eating. It's about embracing the moment we are in and engaging all our senses in the process of nourishing our body during this time.

1. **Start the process of savoring each bite by bringing a mindful presence to the table.** Take a minute to pause and appreciate the meal in front of you, rather than eating on autopilot or while multitasking. Consider the colors, textures, and aromas. Being fully present will help you establish a deeper connection with the food you consume and increase the pleasure you derive from your meal.

2. **Chew Slowly:** The practice of chewing thoughtfully is essential for savoring each meal. Chew your food

slowly and thoroughly, rather than rushing through it. This will help you enjoy the meal more fully. Allow yourself to fully taste each mouthful by paying attention to the flavors and textures you experience during chewing. This not only improves the taste of the food but also aids digestion and leaves you feeling more satisfied after eating.

3. **Gratitude and Appreciation:** Developing an attitude of gratitude for the food on your plate can significantly enhance the eating experience. Take some time to reflect on the journey your food has taken, from its roots in the soil to the hands that prepared it. By expressing thankfulness for the nourishment it provides, you can cultivate a deeper understanding of the interdependence among all beings and the Earth.

4. **The discipline of savoring each bite can be strengthened by incorporating mindful eating rituals into your daily routine.** These rituals can help you become more aware of the present moment. Lighting a candle before meals, reciting a silent blessing, or engaging in a moment of reflection are all examples of simple ways to achieve this goal. These practices are meant to serve as subtle reminders to slow down and enjoy the experience of the moment.

Physical Hunger and Emotional Eating

In a society inundated with external stimuli and cultural pressures, it can be challenging to distinguish between physical hunger and emotional needs. However, it is crucial to pay attention to the cues that signal hunger. Moreover, to cultivate a balanced and intuitive attitude towards eating, it is essential to learn to listen to the signals our body gives us about our hunger.

1. **Developing body awareness** is the first step in deciphering the signals that indicate hunger. Understanding the symptoms you experience, such as stomach rumbling, low energy levels, or a feeling of emptiness, can help identify true physical hunger. On the other hand, if you are aware of specific emotional triggers, such as stress, boredom, or loneliness, you will be better able to differentiate between true hunger and emotional desires that lead to eating not out of hunger but to satisfy a more or less unconscious craving.

2. **Using the hunger scale:** Through the use of the hunger scale, a tool that allows you to assess your state of hunger on a scale from one to ten, you can facilitate the development of mindful eating habits. The goal should be to eat when you feel a comfortable level of hunger (about three or four on the scale from 1 to 10) and to stop eating when you realize you are full but not overly stuffed (7 or 8). This not only prevents mindless overeating but also develops a more attentive

relationship with the hunger signals that the body sends.

3. **It is crucial to intentionally pause before grabbing food,** so you can listen to your body and assess how hungry you are. Evaluate whether you are genuinely hungry or if there are other, less obvious reasons behind your desire to eat. When you give yourself this time for reflection, you have the opportunity to decide what and when to eat, instead of impulsively reacting to external stimuli.

4. **Being aware of our emotions is important,** as our feelings often affect our eating patterns, which can lead to mindless snacking or overeating as a way to cope with stress or discomfort. Through cultivating emotional awareness, you can learn to deal with the feelings that lie beneath the surface and discover other strategies for calming down that do not involve consuming food. To break the pattern of emotional eating, it is helpful to establish healthy coping techniques. Examples of these mechanisms include deep breathing, walking, and creative activities.

What we eat is just one aspect of mindful eating; how we eat is equally important. Our relationship with food can transform from mindless consumption to mindful nourishment if we take the time to savor each bite and pay attention to the indicators that signal when we are hungry. We can create a deeper connection with our body, cultivate a greater appreciation for the food we consume, and ultimately improve our health and overall well-being through the activities we engage in throughout our lives.

Let's continue on the path of mindful eating, one bite at a time, to nourish not just our body but also our soul, so we can nourish ourselves.

Section 4: History and Principles

As a dietary strategy aimed at weight loss and overall health improvement, the practice of intermittent fasting, often termed the "fat-burning method," has surged in popularity in recent years. This is because intermittent fasting is widely considered the most effective method for burning fat. Instead of focusing solely on the types of meals to consume, this eating pattern follows an alternation of fasting and feeding cycles.

This method is more effective than the traditional approach. Its origins date back to ancient rituals, but over time it has been modified and refined to suit modern lifestyles. In this book, we will also discuss the history of intermittent fasting, its principles, how to effectively apply it with the right mindset, the components that contribute to its success, and the reasons why it is effective.

History of Intermittent Fasting

Evidence suggests that intermittent fasting, or abstaining from food, has been practiced for millennia, dating back to ancient civilizations. It has been demonstrated that this practice is beneficial. The practice of intermittent fasting is not a new idea: it has been used for many years and has been passed down from generation to generation. In various nations, throughout history, the practice of fasting has been intertwined with various religious and cultural practices. Purification of the spirit and increased mental clarity are two of its benefits that go beyond the realm of physical health.

Among the earliest documented instances of fasting, one can be traced back to ancient Greece. Pythagoras, the mathematician and philosopher, advocated for periods of time without food consumption to improve physical and mental well-being. In ancient India, the practice of fasting was incorporated into Ayurvedic medicine as a means to purify the body and promote longevity.

Throughout human history, various civilizations and religions, including Buddhism, Judaism, Christianity, and Islam, have observed fasting in various forms. During the holy month of Ramadan, for example, Muslims fast from dawn until sunset. Christians, on the other hand, fast during the period of Lent. Both of these fasting practices are quite distinct from each other.

The modern revival of intermittent fasting can be traced back to the early 20th century when scholars began exploring the potential health benefits of this eating pattern. In the 1930s, researchers like Clive McCay conducted studies on the effects of caloric restriction on the longevity of mice. The findings from these studies laid the groundwork for further investigations into the health implications of fasting.

In the health and wellness field, intermittent fasting has grown in popularity over the last few decades. This movement has been fueled by the growing body of scientific evidence supporting the benefits of intermittent fasting for weight loss, metabolic health, and extending lifespan. Today, it is used by a considerable number of people who are seeking strategies to improve their health and achieve their weight loss goals in a successful and sustainable manner.

Principles of Intermittent Fasting

Intermittent fasting involves alternating periods of eating and fasting, often within a predetermined timeframe. There are several well-known approaches to intermittent fasting, each adopting a different method for selecting the appropriate timing and duration of fasting intervals. Here are some of the most popular methods:

1. **The Leangains protocol**, often known as the 16/8 method, involves limiting food intake to an 8-hour window and abstaining from food for a total of 16 hours per day. For example, one might skip breakfast and consume all meals between noon and 8 PM.

2. **The 5:2 diet** allows individuals to eat regular meals for five days a week, then reduce calorie intake to 500-600 calories on two non-consecutive days.

3. **Alternate day fasting:** As the name suggests, this strategy involves alternating fasting days, where individuals consume a reduced amount of calories or none at all, with non-fasting days, where regular eating resumes.

4. **The Eat-Stop-Eat strategy** involves abstaining from food for a full 24 hours once or twice a week, starting after dinner one day and continuing until dinner the next day.

5. **The Warrior Diet** involves fasting for 20 hours a day and consuming all meals within a four-hour window, typically in the evening.

Regardless of the specific fasting protocol followed, the core idea remains the same: reducing calorie intake for predetermined periods to induce metabolic changes that promote fat burning, weight loss, and other health benefits.

How to Properly Implement Intermittent Fasting with the Right Mindset

To ensure success, intermittent fasting requires adopting healthy behaviors and approaching it with the right mindset. Adopting healthy habits is crucial, even though intermittent fasting can be a useful strategy for weight loss and improving metabolic health. Here are some precautions to follow to properly execute intermittent fasting:

1. **Clearly Define Your Goals.** Before starting an intermittent fasting routine, it's important to clearly establish your goals. Having specific goals can help you maintain motivation and correctly track your progress, whether the goal is to reduce body fat percentage, improve metabolic health, or increase energy levels.

2. **Choose an Appropriate Approach.** Choose a form of intermittent fasting that allows you to achieve your goals while fitting your lifestyle and preferences. When determining which fasting protocol to follow, consider

factors such as your daily routine, work schedules, and personal preferences.

3. **Start Gradually.** If you are new to intermittent fasting, it is advised to start gradually rather than jumping into a strict fasting regimen immediately. It is recommended to gradually increase the time between meals or experiment with shorter fasting periods before moving on to longer ones.

4. **Maintain Proper Hydration.** It is extremely important to stay hydrated during fasting periods. This can be achieved by consuming plenty of water throughout the day. During fasting periods, you may also consume herbal teas, black coffee, and other calorie-free beverages to help suppress hunger and promote hydration.

5. **Nutrient-Dense Meals Are a Priority.** When it is time to eat, it is important to consume whole meals rich in vitamins, minerals, and essential macronutrients. Ensure your meals include a significant amount of fruits, vegetables, lean proteins, healthy fats, and whole grains to nourish your body and support overall health.

6. **Listen to Your Body.** It is crucial to pay attention to your body's signals regarding hunger and energy levels during fasting. If you experience significant discomfort or fatigue, consider adjusting your fasting schedule or consult a nutritionist.

7. **Apply Mindfulness in Real Life.** It is crucial to practice mindful eating when you eat, by chewing slowly, savoring each bite, and observing your body's signals that indicate when it is time to stop eating. By removing distractions such as screens and multitasking while eating, you can develop a deeper connection with the food you are eating and feel more satisfied.

8. **Stay Flexible.** Consistency is the most important factor when achieving benefits with intermittent fasting; however, it is equally important to maintain flexibility and adaptability to manage changes in lifestyle or schedules. If there are specific days when you cannot stick to your fasting schedule, do not worry, just resume your routine as soon as possible without feeling guilty or critical.

9. **Observe Progress.** You can monitor your progress over time by keeping a journal and noting changes in weight, body composition, energy levels, and any other relevant parameters. Recognizing and appreciating even the smallest successes along the way is important to maximize results and ensure long-term success.

10. **Make Overall Health a Priority.** It's important to remember that intermittent fasting is just one component of a healthy lifestyle. It should be complemented by other beneficial behaviors, such as engaging in regular physical activity, getting enough sleep, learning to manage stress effectively, and maintaining social connections. Instead of focusing

solely on weight loss or physical appearance, efforts should be made to improve overall well-being.

If you approach intermittent fasting with the right mindset and form healthy habits, you can benefit from its potential advantages for weight loss, metabolic health, and overall well-being.

Success Factors of Intermittent Fasting The success of intermittent fasting can be attributed to a range of important factors, including its impact on metabolism, hormone management, appetite control, and cellular repair processes. Here are some of the most significant reasons why intermittent fasting is effective:

1. **Metabolic Adaptation:** During fasting periods, the body undergoes a metabolic adaptation process that allows it to conserve energy and stimulate fat burning. Increased insulin sensitivity ensures that cells use glucose more effectively as an energy source, thereby reducing the likelihood of developing insulin resistance and type 2 diabetes.

2. **Hormone Regulation:** Intermittent fasting influences the release of several hormones involved in hunger, satiety, and fat metabolism processes. During fasting periods, levels of ghrelin, also known as the hunger hormone, decrease, helping to suppress appetite and reduce cravings. Conversely, levels of hormones like

insulin, leptin, and adiponectin become more balanced, promoting fat mobilization and energy expenditure.

3. **Increased Fat Oxidation:** Fasting leads the body into a state of ketosis, where it relies on fat reserves for fuel rather than glucose derived from food. The resulting increased fat oxidation facilitates weight loss, particularly in hard-to-lose areas such as the hips and abdomen.

4. **Calorie Restriction:** Intermittent fasting inherently requires calorie restriction during fasting periods, which can lead to a negative energy balance and eventual weight loss over time. Individuals can achieve and maintain a healthy body weight while preserving lean muscle mass through the intentional creation of a persistent caloric deficit.

5. **Autophagy and Cellular Repair:** Fasting is a technique that stimulates autophagy, a cellular cleansing process where damaged or faulty components are broken down and recycled. This not only promotes cell repair but also reduces inflammation and may help prevent age-related cognitive disorders.

6. **Increase in Brain-Derived Neurotrophic Factor (BDNF) and Other Neuroprotective Factors:** Many people who fast report experiencing increased mental clarity, focus, and cognitive functions. This can be attributed to the increased synthesis of BDNF and other neuroprotective factors.

7. **Sustainability and Adherence:** Unlike conventional diets that restrict caloric intake, intermittent fasting offers greater flexibility and simplicity, making it easier for individuals to stick to the diet over a prolonged period. By incorporating fasting into their lifestyle, people can achieve long-term weight loss and improve their metabolic health without feeling deprived or restricted.

8. **Customizable Approach:** Intermittent fasting can be tailored to individual preferences, goals, and metabolic requirements, allowing for specific adjustments based on factors such as age, gender, activity level, and health status. The effectiveness of fasting regimes is enhanced by this customization, which can also lead to better overall results for individuals.

In summary, the effectiveness of intermittent fasting can be attributed to its ability to utilize intrinsic metabolic processes, hormonal control mechanisms, and cellular repair mechanisms in the body. This enables the promotion of fat reduction, improved metabolic health, and enhanced overall well-being.

Often termed the "fat-burning method," intermittent fasting is a nutritional strategy that alternates periods of eating with periods of fasting with the aim of promoting weight loss, improving health and general well-being, and enhancing metabolic health. The practice of intermittent fasting has become increasingly popular as a long-term and successful method for achieving fitness and health goals. Its roots are grounded in ancient practices and a growing number of scientific studies attest to its effectiveness.

With the right mindset, proper behaviors, and an understanding of the fundamentals of intermittent fasting, it can be successfully integrated into one's lifestyle and all its benefits enjoyed. Intermittent fasting promotes long-term health, improves metabolic function, and aids in weight loss. These mechanisms include enhanced fat oxidation and cellular repair, as well as hormonal regulation and metabolic changes.

Like any diet, it is essential to consult a doctor before starting intermittent fasting. This is particularly important if you have dietary restrictions or underlying medical issues. If you follow the right advice and commit to leading a healthy lifestyle, intermittent fasting can be an effective tool to reshape your body and optimize your health for years to come: it is truly a lifestyle. "Intermittent Fasting improves health, overall well-being, and boosts energy. Only as a direct consequence does it cause weight loss. What could be better?"

Section 5: Frequent Asked Questions & Answers

1. **What is intermittent fasting (IF)?** An eating schedule that alternates between times of eating and fasting is known as intermittent fasting.

2. **How does intermittent fasting work?** IF promotes weight loss, enhances metabolic health, and lengthens life by modifying the body's hormone balances.

3. **Is intermittent fasting safe for women over 50?** Yes, women over 50 can safely practice intermittent fasting; but, like with any new diet, it is imperative to speak with a healthcare provider first.

4. **What are the different methods of intermittent fasting?** The Eat-Stop-Eat strategy, the 16/8 method, the 5:2 diet, and alternate-day fasting are examples of popular approaches.

5. **Can intermittent fasting help with weight loss for women over 50?** Yes, by consuming fewer calories and enhancing metabolic health, intermittent fasting can help with weight loss.

6. **What are the potential health benefits of intermittent fasting for women over 50?** Benefits could include decreased inflammation, better insulin sensitivity, weight loss, and improved cognitive function.

7. **Can intermittent fasting help with menopause symptoms?** Some women report improvements in menopause symptoms such as hot flashes and mood swings with intermittent fasting, but more research is needed in this area.

8. **Does intermittent fasting affect hormone levels in women over 50?** Yes, intermittent fasting can impact hormone levels, including insulin, cortisol, and growth hormone, which may have positive effects on health.

9. **Can intermittent fasting help improve cognitive function in women over 50?** Some studies suggest that intermittent fasting may enhance cognitive function and reduce the risk of neurodegenerative diseases.

10. **Is it necessary to count calories while intermittent fasting?** Counting calories is not always necessary with intermittent fasting, but it can be helpful for weight loss goals.

11. **Can I drink water during the fasting period?** Yes, staying hydrated with water, herbal tea, or black coffee is essential during fasting periods.

12. **Are there any foods or beverages that are allowed during fasting periods?** Generally speaking, during fasting periods, calorie-free liquids such as water, black coffee, and unsweetened tea are permitted.

13. **Can I take supplements while intermittent fasting?** As long as the supplements don't include any calories, you can take them while fasting.

14. **Will intermittent fasting cause muscle loss in women over 50?** When combined with resistance training, intermittent fasting can help preserve muscle mass during weight loss.

15. **Is intermittent fasting suitable for women with diabetes or insulin resistance?** Intermittent fasting may help improve insulin sensitivity, but women with diabetes or insulin resistance should consult with a healthcare provider before starting IF.

Section 6: Zero Deprivation Intermittent Fasting Tips

Intermittent fasting has gained popularity due to its effectiveness in weight control, metabolic health improvement, and the prospect of long-term benefits. For intelligent women over fifty, adapting their lifestyle to incorporate intermittent fasting can be a transformative experience. However, it is essential to proceed with caution and customize it according to each person's unique needs and medical conditions. The following recommendations are designed for individuals who are past their forties and wish to incorporate intermittent fasting into their daily routine:

- **Consulting with a doctor before starting a new diet program is essential.** This is particularly important if you are taking medications or have pre-existing health issues. Before beginning, your doctor can provide personalized guidance and ensure that intermittent fasting is suitable and safe for you.

- **If you have never fasted before, you should start with shorter fasts and gradually move to longer fasts** as your body adjusts to the new schedule. One way to do this might be to start with a twelve-hour fast and gradually extend it to fourteen or sixteen hours over time.

- **Choose the correct eating technique:** There are several protocols for intermittent fasting, including the 16/8 approach, which involves fasting for sixteen hours followed by an eight-hour window for eating. The 5:2 method involves five days of regular eating followed by two non-consecutive days of caloric restriction, and alternate-day fasting. To find the strategy that best fits your preferences and lifestyle, you should experiment with different methods.

- **Staying hydrated is essential during fasting:** It's crucial to stay well-hydrated by drinking enough water. Herbal teas, black coffee, and other low-calorie beverages can also help keep you hydrated and feel full for extended periods.

- **When eating, focus on consuming nutrient-rich foods.** These foods should be consumed in large quantities as they are loaded with vitamins, minerals, and antioxidants. It is vital to include a sufficient amount of fruits, vegetables, lean meats, whole grains, and healthy fats in your diet to promote overall health and well-being.

- **It is important to consider the amount of protein intake:** Incorporating sufficient protein in your diet is particularly crucial for women over 50 who want to maintain overall vitality, muscle mass, and bone health. Including lean protein sources in your meals can meet your protein needs. These sources include tofu, beans, lentils, fish, and poultry.

- **Very important: ensure you limit the amount of processed foods, refined carbohydrates, and unhealthy fats in your diet.**
- **Focus on whole, unprocessed foods that provide long-term energy and help you achieve your best health.** Consume a range of fresh fruits and vegetables, lean meats, nuts, seeds, and healthy grains. Thus, arrange these foods on your plate.
- **Observe** how your body reacts to change. If you notice symptoms like fatigue, dizziness, or other negative consequences, it's likely that the fasting process needs adjustment. To ensure your approach aligns with your health and well-being, maintain an open mindset, adapt as necessary, and consult a healthcare professional to ensure it doesn't conflict with any ongoing medical conditions.
- Emphasize **Stress Reduction Techniques** Incorporate stress reduction techniques such as yoga, deep breathing exercises, meditation, and spending time in nature. Managing stress should be a primary goal as prolonged stress can negatively impact hormonal balance and overall health. These methods not only improve general health but can also complement intermittent fasting.
- Focus on **Quality Sleep**. Especially for individuals over 50, getting sufficient sleep is crucial for maintaining hormonal balance, metabolism, and overall health. Establish a regular sleep schedule and aim for seven to

nine hours of quality sleep each night to preserve your body's natural rhythms.
- **Monitor Your Progress**. Keep a **diary** during your fasting journey, where you note the meals consumed, your emotional state during the process, weight outcomes, body measurements, and clothing size. By regularly monitoring your progress, you can identify trends, adjust your approach as needed, and celebrate small victories along the way. So, correct or reward yourself when you deem it appropriate, only you can know.
- Exercise **Perseverance** and **Patience**. Instead of being a quick fix, intermittent fasting is a sustainable lifestyle choice that requires perseverance and consistency. Continue to commit to achieving your goals and remember that progress takes time. Pay homage to even the smallest successes and focus on the long-term benefits of improved health and vitality.

Intermittent fasting is a valuable tool for individuals looking to optimize their health, manage their weight, and enhance overall well-being. By adhering to these recommendations and seeking advice from a healthcare professional, you can safely and successfully integrate intermittent fasting into your lifestyle, and enjoy the numerous benefits it offers.

Section 7: 28-Day Meal Plan for the Busy Woman

The hectic pace of life and overwhelming schedule of commitments often clash with maintaining a balanced diet. To assist you, I'm providing an essential tool to cut down on kitchen time, suitable for meal planning and preparation. A real strategic asset that allows you to have meals prepared and almost ready when needed. A Meal Plan for Busy People can make all the difference and change the game when it comes to maintaining dietary goals and reducing stress, especially amidst a hectic agenda and a multitude of responsibilities. Here are some tips for meal planning and preparation that can help simplify the cooking process and ensure delicious, well-balanced meals throughout the week.

- Batch Cooking: The most crucial aspect of meal preparation is batch cooking. To do so, it's necessary to prepare significant quantities of essential ingredients such as grains, proteins, and vegetables in advance. By preparing these bulk foods, you can drastically reduce the time spent in the kitchen during the week. Additionally, you'll have the necessary components on hand to prepare a wide range of meals.

- It's essential to prepare an ample quantity of grains like rice, quinoa, or pasta so they can be consumed for multiple meals. To ensure they're easily accessible, store them in sealed containers in the refrigerator or freezer. Similarly, prepare large quantities of proteins like chicken, tofu, or beans. To add variety throughout the week, they can be seasoned in various ways.

• Another vital component in batch cooking is vegetables. Prepare your preferred vegetables such as peppers, onions, carrots, and broccoli, and roast them in the oven or sauté them on the stovetop. You can also include broccoli in this mix. Once cooked, divide them into containers to simplify meal assembly.

• Portion Control: Portion control is essential to avoid overeating and maintain a balanced diet. To ensure each meal contains the necessary amounts of proteins, carbohydrates, and fats, it's important to invest in meal preparation tools such as a kitchen scale or portion containers when preparing meals.

• Divide the cooked components into individual portions according to your calorie goals and nutritional requirements. This not only helps control portion sizes but also makes it easier to grab a meal on the go, whether commuting to work or running errands.

• When preparing your meals, aim to fill half of your plate with vegetables, a quarter with lean proteins, and a quarter with complex carbohydrates. This comprehensive strategy ensures the intake of a wide range of nutrients while maintaining control over the quantity of food consumed.

• Adaptable Recipes: When preparing your meals for the week, it's important to choose recipes that are adaptable and can be readily modified to fit your preferences and any health constraints. When searching for recipes, look for ones that require simple, healthy ingredients and allow for modifications or substitutions (refer to the following pages).

• For example, if a dish calls for chicken but you prefer to use tofu or tempeh, feel free to substitute one of these ingredients. Likewise, if you're following a vegetarian or vegan diet, look for recipes that use plant-based proteins like beans, lentils, or tofu. These recipes can be easily converted into meatless versions.

• Similarly, if you have food allergies or intolerances, it's essential to carefully consider the ingredients and make necessary modifications. Many recipes can be adjusted to accommodate dietary restrictions with simple substitutions, such as using dairy-free cheese or gluten-free pasta.

• Choosing flexible recipes allows you to adapt meals to your taste preferences and nutritional needs. This way, you can continue to enjoy delicious and nutritious cuisine.

Meal preparation and planning are extremely useful tools for maintaining a balanced diet and lifestyle. The cooking process can be simplified, time and money can be saved, and you can ensure you have nutritious meals ready to enjoy throughout the week by choosing adaptable recipes, practicing portion control, and cooking in batches. By following these tips, you'll be well on your way to achieving your health and wellness goals.

On the following pages, you'll find a useful meal plan dedicated to all the incredibly busy individuals juggling between family and work.

Having meals ready is essential to reduce stress and achieve dietary goals, especially when navigating a packed schedule that includes family, work, and other responsibilities. This meal plan provides expert tips on how to minimize time spent in the kitchen and explains why meal planning is crucial. By following these guidelines, you can simplify the cooking process and ensure that your meals are delicious and nutritionally balanced throughout the week. You can download and hang the Poster of the following Meal Plan in your kitchen by scanning the QR Code.

If you liked our book, please give us a spontaneous review. It will only take a minute of your time, but it is very important to us.

SCAN THE QRCODE TO DOWNLOAD THE FREE BONUSES

OTHERWISE TYPE IN THIS ADDRESS: https://bit.ly/3Q1U2yo

28-Day Meal Plan for the Busy Woman

DAY	Breakfast	Lunch	Dinner	Snack
1	Avocado and Spinach Omelette	Avocado and Chickpea Salad	Salmon Avocado Salad	Avocado and Tomato Salad
2	Greek Yogurt Parfait	Quinoa and Roasted Vegetable Bowl	Quinoa Stuffed Bell Peppers	Greek Yogurt with Berries
3	Quinoa Breakfast Bowl	Greek Salad with Grilled Chicken	Grilled Lemon Herb Chicken	Cucumber Hummus Bites
4	Smoked Salmon and Avocado Toast	Salmon and Asparagus Foil Packets	Shrimp and Vegetable Stir-Fry	Almond Butter and Banana Rice Cakes
5	Chia Seed Pudding	Turkey and	Turkey and Spinach Stuffed	Caprese Skewers

		Vegetable Stir-Fry	Portobello Mushrooms	
6	Veggie Frittata	Tofu and Veggie Lettuce Wraps	Lentil and Vegetable Soup	Smoked Salmon and Cucumber Rolls
7	Blueberry Almond Smoothie	Cauliflower Fried Rice	Baked Cod with Lemon Herb Sauce	Egg Salad Lettuce Wraps
8	Cottage Cheese with Pineapple	Caprese Zucchini Noodles	Veggie and Tofu Stir-Fry	Zucchini Chips
9	Banana Nut Overnight Oats	Lentil and Vegetable Soup	Eggplant Parmesan	Tuna Stuffed Mini Bell Peppers
10	Spinach and Mushroom Breakfast Wrap	Shrimp and Mango Salad	Chicken and Vegetable Skewers	Cottage Cheese with Pineapple
11	Apple Cinnamon Quinoa Porridge	Eggplant and Tomato Stacks	Butternut Squash and Kale Salad	Walnut and Apple Slices

12	Peanut Butter Banana Smoothie	Chicken and Spinach Salad with Raspberry Vinaigrette	Beef and Broccoli Stir-Fry	Tofu and Vegetable Skewers
13	Berry Protein Pancakes	Tuna and White Bean Salad	Mediterranean Chickpea Salad	Quinoa Salad with Chickpeas
14	Mediterranean Egg Muffins	Ratatouille with Quinoa	Cauliflower Rice Stir-Fry	Roasted Chickpeas
15	Tropical Green Smoothie Bowl	Baked Stuffed Bell Peppers	Greek Yogurt Chicken Salad	Chocolate Covered Strawberries
16	Avocado and Spinach Omelette	Avocado and Chickpea Salad	Salmon Avocado Salad	Avocado and Tomato Salad
17	Greek Yogurt Parfait	Quinoa and Roasted Vegetable Bowl	Quinoa Stuffed Bell Peppers	Greek Yogurt with Berries

18	Quinoa Breakfast Bowl	Greek Salad with Grilled Chicken	Grilled Lemon Herb Chicken	Cucumber Hummus Bites
19	Smoked Salmon and Avocado Toast	Salmon and Asparagus Foil Packets	Shrimp and Vegetable Stir-Fry	Almond Butter and Banana Rice Cakes
20	Chia Seed Pudding	Turkey and Vegetable Stir-Fry	Turkey and Spinach Stuffed Portobello Mushrooms	Caprese Skewers
21	Veggie Frittata	Tofu and Veggie Lettuce Wraps	Lentil and Vegetable Soup	Smoked Salmon and Cucumber Rolls
22	Blueberry Almond Smoothie	Cauliflower Fried Rice	Baked Cod with Lemon Herb Sauce	Egg Salad Lettuce Wraps
23	Cottage Cheese with Pineapple	Lentil and Vegetable Soup	Veggie and Tofu Stir-Fry	Zucchini Chips

24	Banana Nut Overnight Oats	Shrimp and Mango Salad	Eggplant Parmesan	Tuna Stuffed Mini Bell Peppers
25	Spinach and Mushroom Breakfast Wrap	Eggplant and Tomato Stacks	Chicken and Vegetable Skewers	Cottage Cheese with Pineapple
26	Apple Cinnamon Quinoa Porridge	Caprese Zucchini Noodles	Butternut Squash and Kale Salad	Walnut and Apple Slices
27	Peanut Butter Banana Smoothie	Tuna and White Bean Salad	Beef and Broccoli Stir-Fry	Tofu and Vegetable Skewers
28	Berry Protein Pancakes	Ratatouille with Quinoa	Mediterranean Chickpea Salad	Roasted Chickpeas

Section 8: Conclusions

As we are approaching the end of the journey through the pages of "Intermittent Fasting For Smart Women Over 50" it is absolutely necessary to take a few minutes to reflect on the profound discoveries we have made together. Throughout this book, we have:

1. Understood and delved into the nuances of intermittent fasting.
2. Explored the enormous influence it has demonstrated to have on our bodies and our thoughts.
3. Recognized that 90% is mindset, meaning mental attitude, and the remaining 10% is technique, meaning knowledge and actions.
4. Understood the importance of adopting the transformative power of the correct mental attitude.
5. Equipped ourselves adequately with the information and skills necessary to embark on a journey that will lead us to a better and more fulfilled version of ourselves.
6. Acquired in this context the knowledge of the scientific principles underlying fat burning.
7. Now aware that the most important aspect of our inquiry is the realization that achieving the physique we desire is not only a matter of physical effort but also a journey of self-discovery and mental strength, and this awareness is the driving force behind our quest.

8. Also arrived at the realization that true transformation begins from within, with its roots in a change in thought and perception of ourselves.
9. Acknowledge that our bodies are capable of adapting and resiliently resisting.
10. Found the key to long-term weight loss and overall improvement in organism's well-being. This is the secret to our success.
11. The idea that intermittent fasting is a powerful tool for fat burning and optimizing metabolism is one of the fundamental concepts we have embraced. It is one of the core beliefs we have adopted along our journey and is one of the foundational principles we have chosen to embrace.
12. Through the strategic programming of meal timing windows and the incorporation of fasting periods into our routine, we are now able to harness our body's innate ability to burn fat as fuel. Our body composition and overall health have changed significantly as a result.
13. By following the "fat-burning method" of intermittent fasting, we have not only lost the weight we wanted to lose but have also gained a new sense of control and authority over our bodies. Finally, now, we can exercise more freely and vigorously. On the other hand, the profound impact that intermittent fasting has on our mental and emotional well-being is in clear proportion to the substantial benefits it offers in terms of physical health.

14. We have freed ourselves from the chains of restrictive diets and unhealthy eating behaviors by subjecting ourselves to the process of challenging old assumptions about food and nutrition.
15. The practice of mindfulness and intentionality in making decisions about our eating habits has allowed us to cultivate a deeper connection with our bodies and a deeper appreciation for the sustaining power of whole and nutrient-rich foods. This has been possible through the cultivation of a deeper appreciation for the power of whole foods.

The great revelation is that our age will not limit our ability to achieve health and fitness goals, and this factor is an essential and significant component of our journey.

- We are a community of women and men who have surpassed the "forties" and who act intelligently.
- We have embraced the knowledge and experience that come with age and employed them as factors for positive change and personal development.
- We have reconsidered our perspective and changed our mindset to embrace the beauty of aging with grace and confidence.
- This leads to a metamorphosis in our bodies and in how we approach health and wellness.

As we bid farewell to these pages, we carry with us the information and experiences we have gained along the way to further our personal development and gain a greater degree of control over our lives. Just as we learn to recognize the extraordinary encounters that can radically change the journey of life, so do we choose to nourish our bodies with love and care. Let us not forget, above all, that the ability to change is already present in each of us and awaits only to be unleashed with the simple act of believing, having faith, and acting accordingly. As you put this book away and move on to the next part of your journey, it is important to keep the following reminder in mind:

You Are Capable of Achieving What You Believe.

You have the potential to build the life you believe you deserve, a life rich in health, joy, and fulfillment. Enjoy the journey, have faith in the process, and never forget the immense strength that is already within you, especially because, in the end, it is not the place where we are that defines us, but rather the journey we take to get there.

I hope you feel all the excitement I am feeling as I write this farewell. "Intermittent Fasting For Smart Women Over 50" is more than just a book: it is a guide to living a healthier and happier life. In other words, it is a representation of the power that comes from the ability to persevere, to discover oneself, and to believe in oneself.

Furthermore, it reminds us that **aging is not a limit**, but rather an **opportunity to realize our full potential**. For this reason, I would like to toast to you, to myself, and to all the exceptional people, of any age, who have the courage to dream, to believe, and to live.

I sincerely wish that your journey is filled with joy, prosperity, and endless possibilities.

"May you achieve all your goals!"

Annie Kerouak

If you liked our book, please give us a spontaneous review. It will only take a minute of your time, but it is very important to us.

SCAN THE QRCODE TO DOWNLOAD

THE FREE BONUSES

Otherwise Type In This Address: **https://bit.ly/3Q1U2yo**

Section 9: Tasty Recipes

The 90 tasty recipes that follow in the next pages, until the end of the book, are a collection of the best, simple, and nutritious dishes you can find in the international culinary landscape.

These recipes complement and integrate the **28-day Meal Plan** you found in the previous pages and as a downloadable Bonus (a **printable poster** to hang in your kitchen). Additionally, you'll find **65 more recipes as an extra bonus**: 65 photo cards that you can print or consult on your tablet, smartphone, or personal computer.

All of this is dedicated to super busy people like you and structured in a way that can help simplify your life.

Tasty Breakfast Recipes

1. Avocado and Spinach Omelette

- Five minutes for preparation
- Cooking Period: 10 minutes
- Serves: One

Ingredients:

- two eggs
- sliced 1/4 avocado, handful of spinach
- To taste, add salt and pepper.

Directions:

1. In a bowl, whisk together the eggs and add salt and pepper to taste (this step is optional).
2. The eggs should be placed in a skillet that does not stick to the pan, and then the skillet should be heated over medium heat.
3. Once the sides have started to firm, it is time to finish the dish by adding the avocado slices and spinach.
4. The omelette should be cooked until it reaches the proper consistency, after which it should be folded in half and served.

Nutritional Information:

- Total: kCal: 278 Protein: 15g Fat: 21g Carbs: 5g

2. Greek Yogurt Parfait

- Five minutes for preparation
- Serves: One

Ingredients:

- One-fourth cup of Greek yogurt
- Half a cup of mixed berries
- 1 tbsp almond slices
- Drizzle of honey (optional)

Directions:

1. Greek yogurt, mixed berries, and almond pieces should be layered layer by layer in a glass or bowl.
2. You can drizzle honey on top if you like.
3. Serve as soon as possible.

Nutritional Information:

- Total: kCal: 220 Protein: 18g Fat: 11g Carbs: 15g

3. Quinoa Breakfast Bowl

- Five minutes for preparation
- Cooking Period: 15 minutes
- Serves: Two

Ingredients:

- Half a cup of rinsed quinoa and one cup of water or almond milk
- One-half teaspoon of cinnamon
- nuts (almonds, walnuts, or pecans) chopped to a quarter cup level
- One-fourth of a cup of dried fruit, such as raisins, cranberries, or apricots

Directions:

1. Cinnamon, water or almond milk, and quinoa should be combined in a bowl or another container and stirred together.
2. The quinoa should be cooked for a further fifteen minutes, or until it is soft, depending on when it boils. Reduce the heat to a simmer after that.
3. Following the completion of the cooking process, the quinoa should be plated in individual dishes and topped with chopped nuts and dried fruit.
4. Serve while the food is still hot.

Nutritional Information:

- Total: kCal: 285 Protein: 8g Fat: 12g Carbs: 38g

4. Smoked Salmon and Avocado Toast

- Prep Time: 5 min
- Serves: 1

Ingredients:

- A single slice of whole grain toast

- Two ounces of smoked salmon
- 1/4 avocado, mashed, with juice from lemon
- To taste, add more salt and pepper.

Directions:

1. On top of the bread that has been toasted, spread the avocado that has been mashed.
2. Add some smoked salmon on the top of the dish.
3. Salt and pepper should be used to season the topping, and fresh lemon juice should be drizzled over it before serving.
4. Serve as quickly as you possibly can.

Nutritional Information:

- Total: kCal: 254 Protein: 21g Fat: 10g Carbs: 18g

5. Chia Seed Pudding

- Prep Time: 5 min (+overnight chilling)
- Serves: 2

Ingredients:

- 25% of the chia seed cup
- A single cup of almond milk
- Vanilla extract, one teaspoon
- Honey or maple syrup, one tablespoon;
- for use as a topping, fresh berries

Directions:

1. In a bowl, mix together the chia seeds, almond milk, vanilla extract, honey, or maple syrup. Stir the mixture until all of the ingredients are well incorporated.
2. After covering and refrigerating for at least three hours, or overnight, until the mixture has thickened.
3. Use fresh berries as a topping for the dish.

Nutritional Information:

- Total: kCal: 140 Protein: 4g Fat: 7g Carbs: 18g

6. Veggie Frittata

- Ten minutes for preparation
- Cooking Duration: 20 minutes
- Serves: 4.

Ingredients:

- Six eggs
- chopped bell peppers, half a cup
- a half-cup of chopped mushrooms, finely
- a quarter cup of onions, chopped finely
- a little handful of spinach
- To taste, add salt and pepper.

Directions:

1. Preheat the oven to 175 degrees Celsius, or 350 degrees Fahrenheit.
2. Transfer the eggs to a bowl and stir in the salt and pepper.
3. Stir in the diced veggies after adding them.
4. Transfer the contents to an ovenproof skillet that has been greased.
5. Bake the frittata for twenty minutes, or until it has set and has a golden brown color.
6. Kindly cut and present.

Nutritional Information:

- Total: kCal: 156 Protein: 11g Fat: 10g Carbs: 5g

7. Blueberry Almond Smoothie

- Five minutes for preparation

- Serves: 1

Ingredients:

- half a cup of blueberries, either fresh or frozen
- One-half banana and one-quarter cup almond milk
- One spoonful of butter made of almonds
- A quarter of a cup Greek yogurt

Directions:

1. Process all the ingredients in a blender until very smooth.
2. Serve right away.

Nutritional Information:

- Total: kCal: 268 Protein: 15g Fat: 10g Carbs: 34g

8. Cottage Cheese with Pineapple

- Prep Time: 5 min
- Serves: 1

Ingredients:

- one-half cup cottage cheese
- half a cup of pineapple, chopped
- One tablespoon of chopped nuts, optional

Directions:

1. Mix the cottage cheese and pineapple that has been chopped together in a bowl.
2. However, if you so wish, sprinkle with chopped nuts.
3. To be served cold.

Nutritional Information:

- Total: kCal: 186 Protein: 20g Fat: 4g Carbs: 18g

9. Banana Nut Overnight Oats

- Prep Time: 5 min (+overnight chilling)
- Serves: 1

Ingredients:

- One-half cup rolled oats
- One-half cup almond milk
- A half-ripe banana, mashed;
- one tablespoon of chopped nuts (almonds or walnuts)
- A drizzle of maple syrup or honey is optional.

Directions:

1. Put the rolled oats, almond milk, mashed banana, and chopped nuts into a jar or another container and mix them together.
2. For the night, cover and store in the refrigerator.
3. In the morning, give the mixture a good stir, and feel free to top it with some maple syrup or honey.

Nutritional Information:

- Total: kCal: 320 Protein: 10g Fat: 12g Carbs: 45g

10. Spinach and Mushroom Breakfast Wrap

- Five minutes for preparation
- Cooking Period: 5 minutes
- Serves: One

Ingredients:

- 1 large whole grain tortilla
- Handful of spinach
- 1/4 cup sliced mushrooms
- 2 eggs, scrambled
- Cheese that has been shredded to a quarter cup
- Salt and pepper should be added to taste.

Directions:

1. Warm the tortilla in a skillet over a heat setting of medium.
2. Using the tortilla, layer the following ingredients: spinach, mushrooms, scrambled eggs, and shredded cheese.
3. Use pepper and salt to season the food.
4. The tortilla should be rolled up and served warm.

Nutritional Information:

- Total: kCal: 340 Protein: 20g Fat: 18g Carbs: 25g

11. Apple Cinnamon Quinoa Porridge

- Five minutes for preparation
- Cooking Duration: 20 minutes
- Serves: Two

Ingredients:

- One cup of water or almond milk, together with half a cup of quinoa that has been washed.
- One chopped apple
- Half a teaspoon of cinnamon
- Honey or maple syrup, one tablespoon;

Directions:

1. Quinoa, water or almond milk, sliced apples, cinnamon, and either maple syrup or honey should all be combined in a saucepan.
2. When it reaches a boil, turn the heat down to a simmer and continue cooking for another twenty minutes, or until the apples have become crisp and the quinoa has reached the desired desired tenderness.
3. While still warm, serve.

Nutritional Information:

- Total: kCal: 282 Protein: 7g Fat: 4g Carbs: 55g

12. Peanut Butter Banana Smoothie

- The preparation time is five minutes.
- Serves: 1

Ingredients:

- Singularly one banana
- One tablespoon of peanut butter is required.
- almond milk, one-half cup quantity
- one-fourth cup Greek yogurt
- Scoop of ice cubes

Directions:

1. All of the components should be blended together in a blender until they are completely transparent. This will be the preparation of the mixture.
2. Serve as quickly as you possibly can.

Nutritional Information:

- Total: kCal: 292 Protein: 14g Fat: 14g Carbs: 32g

13. Berry Protein Pancakes

- Ten minutes for preparation
- Cooking Period: 10 minutes
- Serves: Two

Ingredients:

- One cup of rolled oats
- One ripe banana
- two eggs
- One-half cup of a variety of berries
- One-half of a teaspoon of extract of vanilla
- A half-tsp of baking powder

Directions:

1. Put the rolled oats, banana, eggs, vanilla extract, and baking powder into a blender and thoroughly mix them together.
2. Blend until it is completely smooth.
3. Prepare a skillet that does not stick by heating it over medium heat.
4. Pour batter onto the skillet over medium heat to make pancakes.
5. Mix with a handful of different berries.
6. After the food starts to bubble on the surface, turn it over and cook it for a further few minutes until it turns golden brown.
7. While still warm, serve.

Nutritional Information:

- Total: kCal: 265 Protein: 12g Fat: 6g Carbs: 42g

14. Mediterranean Egg Muffins

- Ten minutes for preparation
- Cooking Duration: 20 minutes
- Serves: 4.

Ingredients:

- Six eggs
- a quarter cup of tomatoes that have been chopped
- You will need a quarter cup of chopped spinach and a quarter cup of crumbled feta cheese.
- To taste, add salt and pepper.

Directions:

1. Bake at a temperature of 175 degrees Celsius (350 degrees Fahrenheit) in a muffin tray that has been greased.
2. The eggs, diced tomatoes, chopped spinach, crumbled feta cheese, and salt and pepper should be mixed together in a bowl using a whisk. The ingredients should also be combined with the diced tomatoes.
3. If you are using muffin cups, make sure that the egg mixture is distributed equally.
4. The egg muffins should be baked for twenty minutes, or until they have reached the desired consistency and have a golden finish.
5. Let the mixture cool down a little bit before removing it from the tin.
6. Warm or at room temperature, serve as desired.

Nutritional Information:

- Total: kCal: 120 Protein: 10g Fat: 7g Carbs: 4g

15. Tropical Green Smoothie Bowl

- Prep Time: 5 min
- Serves: 1

Ingredients:

- One banana, frozen
- a half cup of pineapple pieces that have been frozen
- small bunch of spinach in a handful
- a half cup of water made from coconut
- Toppers: shredded coconut, sliced kiwi, and chia seeds

Directions:

1. In a blender, combine the frozen banana, frozen pineapple chunks, spinach, and coconut water; process until well incorporated.
2. Puree till it is silky smooth and creamy.
3. To finish, add sliced kiwi, shredded coconut, and chia seeds to the top of the bowl after it has been poured.
4. Serve as soon as possible.

Nutritional Information:

- Total: kCal: 210 Protein: 4g Fat: 1g Carbs: 52g

Satisfying Lunch Recipes

16. Avocado and Chickpea Salad

- Ten minutes for preparation
- Cooking Period: 0 minutes
- Serves: Two

Ingredients:

- one diced ripe avocado
- One cup of cooked lentils
- 1/2 chopped cucumber and 1/4 thinly sliced red onion
- Two tablespoons of lemon juice
- One tablespoon of olive oil
- To taste, add salt and pepper.

Directions:

1. It is recommended that all of the components, which include the avocado, chickpeas, cucumber, and red onion, be mixed together in a large bowl or dish.
2. To complete the salad, drizzle it with olive oil and lemon juice that has been freshly squeezed.
3. Immediately after seasoning with salt and pepper, combine the ingredients by gently tossing them together.
4. To be served in a freezer.

Serving Total:

- kCal: 230 Protein: 7g Fat: 15g Carbs: 20g

17. Quinoa and Roasted Vegetable Bowl

- It takes fifteen minutes to prepare.
- Twenty-five minutes is the cooking time.

- Two servings

Ingredients:

- One cup of cooked quinoa
- One little sweet potato, chopped
- half a cup of cherry tomatoes
- Sliced bell peppers, half a cup
- 1/4 cup of red onion, chopped
- Two tsp olive oil
- 1tsp paprika smoked
- To taste, add salt and pepper.

Directions:

1. Adjust the temperature of the oven to 200 degrees Celsius, which is equivalent to 400 degrees Fahrenheit.
2. Before putting the baking sheet into the oven, apply a mixture of olive oil, smokey paprika, salt, and pepper to the sweet potato, cherry tomatoes, bell peppers, and red onion. Toss the ingredients together.
3. Bake the vegetables for twenty to twenty-five minutes, or until they are soft.
4. Once the quinoa has cooked, transfer it to bowls and sprinkle some roasted vegetables over top.
5. While still warm, serve.

Serving Total:

- kCal: 315 Protein: 7g Fat: 12g Carbs: 45g

18. Greek Salad with Grilled Chicken

- The preparation time is fifteen minutes.
- ten minutes for cooking
- Servings: two

Ingredients:

- A couple of chicken breasts
- two cups of mixed greens
- One chopped cucumber
- one cup of cherry tomatoes cut in half
- 1/4 of a thinly sliced red onion
- One-fourth cup of kalamata olives
- Two tbsp finely chopped feta cheese
- A couple of tablespoons of olive oil
- A single spoonful of vinegar made from red wine
- A single tsp of dehydrated oregano
- Season with salt and pepper.

Directions:

1. Season the chicken breasts with a pinch of salt, a sprinkle of pepper, and some dried oregano. Cook for approximately 4 to 5 minutes on each side, or until the meat is cooked through.
2. In a big basin, combine the kalamata olives, cucumber, cherry tomatoes, feta cheese, mixed greens, and red onion.
3. Toss the salad to blend after adding the red wine vinegar and olive oil.
4. Serve the salad topped with grilled chicken slices.
5. Quickly prepare and serve.

Serving Total:

- kCal: 380 Protein: 30g Fat: 20g Carbs: 20g

19. Salmon and Asparagus Foil Packets

- Ten minutes for preparation
- Cooking Duration: 20 minutes
- Serves: Two

Ingredients:

- Two fillets of salmon
- One cut bunch of asparagus
- Two tablespoons of lemon juice
- Two cloves of chopped garlic and two teaspoons of olive oil
- To taste, add salt and pepper.

Directions:

1. A temperature of 400 degrees Fahrenheit (200 degrees Celsius) should be reached in the oven.
2. It is recommended that each salmon fillet be placed on a sheet of foil that is sufficiently large to allow it to be folded over and sealed on the very edge.
3. Around each and every salmon fillet, asparagus should be put in a circular pattern.
4. After the salmon and asparagus have been prepared, drizzle them with olive oil, lemon juice, and garlic that has been minced.
5. Both pepper and salt should be used to season the food.
6. The salmon and asparagus should be folded over the foil, and the edges should be sealed tightly.
7. Bake the salmon in an oven that has been warmed for fifteen to twenty minutes, or until it is completely cooked through.
8. Warm the dish.

Serving Total:

- kCal: 290 Protein: 30g Fat: 15g Carbs: 10g

20. Turkey and Vegetable Stir-Fry

- Ten minutes for preparation
- Cooking Period: 15 minutes

- Serves: Two

Ingredients:

- One tablespoon of olive oil
- 1/2 pound of finely sliced turkey breast
- One sliced bell pepper and one cup of broccoli florets
- One chopped carrot and two minced garlic cloves
- Two tablespoons of soy sauce
- One teaspoon of sesame oil
- One teaspoon honey
- Sunflower seeds as a garnish

Directions:

1. Heat the olive oil in a large skillet over medium-high heat.
2. To brown the turkey breast slices, add them and continue to cook for around three to four minutes.
3. Place the bell pepper, broccoli, carrot, and garlic that has been minced into the skillet or pan.
4. Fry the veggies in a pan for about five or six minutes, or until they're just slightly softened.
5. Honey, sesame oil, and soy sauce should be mixed together in a small basin using a whisk.
6. Before tossing the turkey and veggies to coat them, pour the sauce over them.
7. Simmer the meal for a further minute or two, or until it is heated through.
8. Sesame seeds are used as a garnish. before serving.

Serving Total:

- kCal: 280 Protein: 25g Fat: 10g Carbs: 20g

21. Tofu and Veggie Lettuce Wraps

- 15 minutes for preparation
- Cooking Period: 10 minutes
- Serves: Two

Ingredients:

- One brick of firm tofu, crushed and drained
- One cup of sliced mushrooms,
- one diced bell pepper
- half a cup of shredded carrots
- Two sliced green onions
- two minced garlic cloves
- Two tablespoons of soy sauce
- One tablespoon of hoisin sauce
- One teaspoon of sesame oil
- Leaves of butter lettuce to wrap

Directions:

1. To begin, place a skillet over medium heat with the sesame oil.
2. Cook for three to four minutes, or until gently browned, after adding the crumbled tofu.
3. The mushrooms, bell pepper, shredded carrots, green onions, and minced garlic should all be added to the hot skillet.
4. Stir-fry the vegetables for an additional three to four minutes, or until they are tender.
5. Put the hoisin sauce and soy sauce in a small bowl and mix them together.
6. The tofu and vegetables should be mixed together after the sauce has been poured over them.
7. Spoon the mixture of tofu and vegetables onto the butter lettuce leaves.

8. Serve right away.

Serving Total:

- kCal: 220 Protein: 20g Fat: 10g Carbs: 15g

22. Cauliflower Fried Rice

- Ten minutes for preparation
- Cooking Period: 15 minutes
- Serves: Two

Ingredients:

- Grated half a head of cauliflower and two beaten eggs
- One cup of mixed veggies (corn, carrots, and peas)
- Two sliced green onions and two minced garlic cloves
- Soy sauce, two tablespoons
- An ounce of sesame oil
- Season with salt and pepper to taste.

Directions:

1. Heat the sesame oil to a medium heat in a big skillet.
2. Chop the green onions and garlic and sauté them for a minute or two until they unleash their aroma.
3. Transfer the garlic and onions to one side of the skillet and pour the beaten eggs into the other.
4. Stir the eggs with the garlic and onions after scrambling them until they are completely cooked through.
5. To the skillet, add cauliflower that has been grated and a variety of veggies.
6. For five to six minutes, stir-fry the cauliflower until it is soft.
7. The cauliflower fried rice should be tossed with soy sauce once it has been poured over it.
8. Add salt and pepper to taste, and season with salt.

9. Warm the dish.

Serving Total:

- kCal: 180 Protein: 10g Fat: 8g Carbs: 20g

23. Caprese Zucchini Noodles

- Ten minutes for preparation
- Cooking Period: 0 minutes
- Serves: Two

Ingredients:

- Twirled two medium zucchinis
- One cup of halved cherry tomatoes
- A half-cup of newly made mozzarella sticks
- 1/4 cup of freshly chopped basil
- Dollop of balsamic glaze
- two tsp olive oil
- To taste, add more salt and pepper.

Directions:

1. Combine spiralized zucchini noodles, torn basil leaves, cherry tomatoes, and fresh mozzarella balls in a big bowl.
2. Drizzle the zucchini noodle mixture with balsamic glaze and olive oil before serving.
3. Gently mix the ingredients together after adding the salt and pepper.
4. to be served cold.

Serving Total:

- kCal: 220 Protein: 8g Fat: 15g Carbs: 15g

24. Lentil and Vegetable Soup

- Ten Minutes for Prep
- 30-Minute Cooking Time
- Contains: 4 servings

Ingredients:

- One cup of rinsed and dried lentil
- four cups of vegetable broth
- one onion; two carrots; two celery stalks; two chopped chopped garlic cloves
- One tsp of thyme, dried
- One tsp of rosemary, dried
- To taste, add salt and pepper.
- As a garnish, use fresh parsley.

Directions:

1. The lentils, the vegetable broth, the diced onion, the carrots, the celery, the minced garlic, the dried thyme, and the dried rosemary should all be combined in a large saucepan with the other ingredients.
2. If you want your lentils and veggies cooked to perfection, boil the ingredients for a few minutes, then reduce heat to low and simmer for another 25–30 minutes.
3. Add pepper and salt to taste, and season with salt when you are done.
4. Served hot, with a topping of fresh herbs and condiments. It is parsley.

Serving Total:

- kCal: 180 Protein: 10g Fat: 1g Carbs: 35g

25. Shrimp and Mango Salad

- Time Required for Preparation: fifteen minutes
- Duration: 5 minutes
- Two servings

Ingredients:

- Peeled and deveined shrimp weighing one pound
- a mango, diced
- an avocado, diced
- a quarter of a red onion cut thinly
- a quarter cup of chopped cilantro
- two tablespoons of lime juice
- olive oil, one tablespoon
- Add salt and pepper to taste.

Directions:

1. In a skillet over medium-high heat, bring the olive oil to a simmer.
2. The shrimp should be cooked for two or three minutes per side once added to the pan, or until they turn pink and have a good amount of flesh.
3. A big bowl should be used to combine chopped amounts of mango, avocado, red onion, and cilantro. The ingredients should be combined together.
4. When you have finished adding the lime juice and olive oil to the salad, give it a light toss so that all of the components are incorporated.
5. Once the shrimp are cooked, add them to the salad and season with salt and pepper.
6. For quick assistance, please.

Serving Total:

- kCal: 280 Protein: 30g Fat: 10g Carbs: 20g

26. Eggplant and Tomato Stacks

- Ten minutes for preparation
- Cooking Duration: 20 minutes
- Serves: Two

Ingredients:

- 1 eggplant of considerable size, cut into rounds
- 2 tomatoes, cut into slices
- Half a cup of sliced fresh mozzarella
- One-fourth cup of fresh basil leaves
- Balsamic glaze, two tablespoons
- Using two teaspoons of olive oil
- Add salt and pepper according to your preference.

Directions:

1. Get the oven up to 200 degrees Celsius (400 degrees Fahrenheit).
2. Season the eggplant slices with salt and pepper after coating them in olive oil for the perfect flavor.
3. Roast the eggplant slices for fifteen to twenty minutes after placing them on a baking pan. The eggplant will remain tender if you do this.
4. The dish should be removed from the oven and allowed to cool for a little period of time.
5. Create stacks of eggplant and tomatoes by placing slices of eggplant, slices of tomato, slices of fresh mozzarella, and basil leaves in a specific order.
6. The stacks should be covered with a glaze that is made of balsamic vinegar.
7. Serve while the food is still hot.

Serving Total:

- kCal: 250 Protein: 10g Fat: 15g Carbs: 25g

27. Chicken and Spinach Salad with Raspberry Vinaigrette

- Ten minutes for preparation
- Cooking Period: 10 minutes
- Serves: Two

Ingredients:

- Two breasts of chicken
- The baby spinach, four cups
- one-half cup of raspberries
- half a cup of almonds, sliced
- 2 tablespoons of olive oil
- Balsamic vinegar, two tablespoons
- Dijon mustard, one teaspoon
- To taste, season with salt and pepper

Directions:

1. Salt and pepper are the right seasonings to use on chicken breasts. Cook the meat for around four or five minutes per side on the grill until it's done.
2. A large bowl should be used to combine baby spinach, raspberries, and almonds that have been sliced into smaller pieces.
3. In a small bowl, mix together the olive oil, balsamic vinegar, Dijon mustard, salt, and pepper to make the vinaigrette. The vinaigrette is ready to use at this time.
4. To finish off the salad, slice the chicken that has been grilled and arrange it in a decorative pattern.
5. Vinaigrette that has been created using raspberry juice should be used to dress the salad.
6. Serve as quickly as you possibly can.

Serving Total: kCal: 320 Protein: 30g Fat: 15g Carbs: 15g

28. Tuna and White Bean Salad

- Ten minutes for preparation
- Cooking Period: 0 minutes
- Serves: Two

Ingredients:

- Two tuna cans, drained
- One can of washed and drained white beans
- Dice 1/2 red bell pepper and 1/4 red onion.
- A generous pinch of coarsely chopped parsley
- Lemon juice in two tablespoons
- Two tsp olive oil
- To taste, add more salt and pepper.

Directions:

1. In a large bowl, combine the tuna that has been drained, the white beans, the diced bell pepper, the diced red onion, and the chopped parsley.
2. To end, drizzle olive oil and lemon juice over the salad.
3. Gently mix the ingredients together after adding the salt and pepper.
4. to be served cold.

Serving Total:

- kCal: 250 Protein: 25g Fat: 10g Carbs: 15g

29. Ratatouille with Quinoa

- 15 minutes for preparation
- Cooking Duration: 30 minutes
- Serves: 4.

Ingredients:

- 1 eggplant, diced

- 2 zucchinis, diced
- One diced onion
- one diced bell pepper
- two minced garlic cloves
- two cups diced tomatoes
- One teaspoon of dried thyme
- Dried oregano, one teaspoon
- 2 cups of quinoa to be cooked
- To taste, season with salt and pepper
- Fresh basil for garnish

Directions:

1. Olive oil should be added to a large skillet that is being heated over medium heat.
2. After the skillet has reached the desired temperature, add the chopped zucchini, bell pepper, onion, and garlic.
3. It should take about five to six minutes for the vegetables to become tender after they are sautéed.
4. Combine the chopped tomatoes, dried thyme, and dried oregano by hand and stir until combined.
5. Turn the heat down to low and let the mixture simmer for fifteen to twenty minutes, or until all of the flavors have amalgamated completely.
6. Add pepper and salt to taste, and season with salt.
7. Place the cooked quinoa on top of the ratatouille.
8. Just before serving, garnish with some fresh basil. helping.

Serving Total:

- kCal: 280 Protein: 8g Fat: 10g Carbs: 40g

30. Baked Stuffed Bell Peppers

- Prep Time: 15 min
- Cook Time: 25 min
- Serves: 2

Ingredients:

- Two bell peppers, seeded and cut in half
- One cup of cooked quinoa
- The amount of black beans, rinsed and drained, is one cup.
- Corn kernels, one cup in total
- half a cup of salsa
- a half cup of cheddar cheese that has been shredded
- Tbsp finely chopped cilantro
- To taste, add salt and pepper.

Directions:

1. Adjust the temperature of the oven to 375 degrees Fahrenheit (190 degrees Celsius).
2. Mix the quinoa that has been cooked, the black beans, the corn kernels, the salsa, the shredded cheddar cheese, the chopped cilantro, and the seasonings (salt and pepper) in a separate big bowl.
3. Place a heaping tablespoon of the quinoa mixture inside of each half of the bell pepper.
4. After the bell peppers have been packed, place them in a roasting dish.
5. The dish should be covered with aluminum foil and placed inside the oven once the oven has been preheated for twenty minutes.
6. Remove the top and continue baking for an additional five minutes, or until the cheese has melted and begun to bubble like it did before.

7. Warm up the meal again.

Serving Total:

- kCal: 320 Protein: 15g Fat: 10g Carbs: 45g

Nutrient-Dense Dinners:

31. Salmon Avocado Salad

- Ten minutes for preparation
- Cooking Period: 15 minutes
- Serves: Two

Ingredients:

- Two salmon fillets
- two servings of mixed greens
- 1/4 cup of cherry tomatoes, halved
- a single avocado slice
- 1/4 cup of cucumbers, sliced
- Two tsp olive oil
- One tsp lemon juice
- Add salt and pepper to taste.

Directions:

1. Bring the oven temperature up to 375 °F, or 190 °C. Season the salmon fillets with salt and pepper, then bake them for fifteen minutes, or until they are opaque throughout.
2. Combine the mixed greens, avocado, cherry tomatoes, and cucumber in a large bowl.
3. Combine the olive oil and lemon juice in a bowl and whisk to create the dressing.

4. To serve, arrange the roasted salmon on top of the salad and drizzle with the lemon dressing.

Nutritional Information (per serving):

- Total: kCal: 325 Protein: 25g Fat: 22g Carbs: 10g

32. Quinoa Stuffed Bell Peppers

- 15 minutes for preparation
- Cooking Duration: 30 minutes
- Serves: 4.

Ingredients:

- Four bell peppers
- One cup of cooked quinoa
- One can of black beans that have been rinsed and drained
- A single cup of corn kernels
- 1/2 cup of chopped tomatoes
- Finely cut 1/4 cup of cilantro.
- A single teaspoon of cumin
- Chilli powder, 1/2 teaspoon
- Season with pepper and salt to taste.
- If preferred, add a half-cup of shredded cheese.

Directions:

1. Bring the oven temperature up to 375 °F, or 190 °C. Take the bell peppers and remove their seeds. Then, slice off their tops.
2. An enormous bowl is the place to mix cooked quinoa, black beans, corn, tomatoes, cilantro, cumin, chili powder, salt, and pepper.

3. In a baking dish, stuff the bell peppers with the quinoa mixture and bake them. If you choose, you can sprinkle some shredded cheese on top.
4. Bake peppers until soft, about 20 to 30 minutes.

Nutritional Information (per serving):

- Total: kCal: 280 Protein: 11g Fat: 3g Carbs: 55g

33. Grilled Lemon Herb Chicken

- Ten minutes for preparation
- Cooking Duration: 20 minutes
- Serves: Two

Ingredients:

- Two breasts of chicken
- Two tablespoons of olive oil
- two minced garlic cloves
- One lemon, squeezed and sliced
- One teaspoon of dried thyme
- One teaspoon dried rosemary
- To taste, add salt and pepper.

Directions:

1. Turn the grill to medium-high heat.
2. A little bowl is all you need to blend the olive oil, minced garlic, lemon juice, zest, thyme, rosemary, salt, and pepper.
3. Stuff the chicken breasts with the herb mixture.
4. To ensure that the chicken is cooked through, grill it for ten to twelve minutes on each side.

Nutritional Information (per serving):

- Total: kCal: 280 Protein: 25g Fat: 12g Carbs: 5g

34. Shrimp and Vegetable Stir-Fry

- 15 minutes for preparation
- Cooking Period: 10 minutes
- Serves: Two

Ingredients:

- One pound of peeled and deveined shrimp
- Two cups of mixed veggies, including snap peas, broccoli, and bell peppers
- two minced garlic cloves
- a pair of teaspoons soy sauce
- Sesame oil, one tablespoon
- 1 tsp grated ginger
- Two green onion
- chopped sesame seeds (optional)

Directions:

1. With the heat set to medium-high, warm the sesame oil in a big skillet.
2. Mince the garlic and finely grate the ginger. Heat the mixture for one minute.
3. Throw in the veggies and shrimp, and stir them around frequently in the pan. Make sure the shrimp and veggies are cooked until they're tender and pink.
4. After adding the soy sauce, stir and cook for an extra two minutes.
5. Just before serving, sprinkle with sliced green onions and toasted sesame seeds.

Nutritional Information (per serving):

- Total: kCal: 280 Protein: 35g Fat: 7g Carbs: 15g

35. Turkey and Spinach Stuffed Portobello Mushrooms

- 15 minutes for preparation
- Cooking Duration: 25 minutes
- Serves: Two

Ingredients:

- 2 large Portobello mushrooms
- 1/2 lb ground turkey
- 2 cups spinach, chopped
- one-fourth cup finely chopped onions
- two minced garlic cloves
- 1/4 cup of Parmesan cheese, grated
- 1 tsp of Italian spice
- To taste, add salt and pepper.

Directions:

1. A temperature of 375 degrees Fahrenheit (190 degrees Celsius) should be reached in the oven. The gills of the Portobello mushrooms should be removed using a spoon once the stems have been removed from the mushrooms.
2. Ground turkey should be cooked in a pan over medium heat until it appears to have a browned appearance.
3. The garlic that has been minced and the onion that has been diced should be added to the skillet once the items have reached the desired tenderness.
4. Chopped spinach, Italian seasoning, salt, and pepper should be stirred in at this point. Prepare the spinach until it wilts.
5. After carefully stuffing each mushroom cap with the turkey and spinach mixture, sprinkle the mushroom caps with grated Parmesan cheese.

6. For twenty to twenty-five minutes, bake the mushrooms until they are soft and the cheese has melted.

Nutritional Information (per serving):

- Total: kCal: 240 Protein: 28g Fat: 9g Carbs: 15g

36. Lentil and Vegetable Soup

- Ten minutes for preparation
- Cooking Duration: 30 minutes
- Serves: 4.

Ingredients:

- 4 cups of veggie broth
- 1 cup of washed dried lentils
- One onion
- two chopped carrots
- two diced celery stalks
- two diced garlic cloves
- one tsp of minced cumin
- One teaspoon of paprika
- To taste, add salt and pepper.
- As a garnish, use fresh parsley.

Directions:

1. Combine the lentils, vegetable broth, chopped celery, carrots, and onion with the minced garlic, cumin, paprika, salt, and pepper in a big pot.
2. After the mixture has to a boil, reduce the heat to a simmer and continue cooking for an additional 25 to 30 minutes, or until the lentils and vegetables have reached the desired level of tenderness.
3. Decorate the dish with fresh parsley while it is still hot, and then serve.

Nutritional Information (per serving):

- Total: kCal: 220 Protein: 15g Fat: 1g Carbs: 40g

37. Baked Cod with Lemon Herb Sauce

- Ten minutes for preparation
- Cooking Duration: 20 minutes
- Serves: Two

Ingredients:

- Two fillets of cod
- Two tablespoons of olive oil
- two minced garlic cloves
- One lemon, squeezed and sliced
- One teaspoon of dried thyme
- One teaspoon of dried parsley
- To taste, add salt and pepper.

Directions:

1. A temperature of 375 degrees Fahrenheit (190 degrees Celsius) should be reached in the oven. Using a baking dish, arrange the fish fillets in a single layer.
2. Combine the following ingredients in a small bowl: olive oil, garlic that has been minced, lemon juice, lemon zest, thyme, parsley, salt, and pepper.
3. After ensuring that the cod fillets are evenly coated with the herb mixture, pour it over them and put them aside.
4. Bake the fish for 15 to 20 minutes, or until a fork can easily pierce it.

Nutritional Information (per serving):

- Total: kCal: 200 Protein: 25g Fat: 10g Carbs: 2g

38. Veggie and Tofu Stir-Fry

- 15 minutes for preparation
- Cooking Period: 15 minutes
- Serves: Two

Ingredients:

- Tofu in the form of a little block
- the equivalent of two cups of a variety of veggies, including broccoli, carrots, and bell peppers
- two minced garlic cloves
- Two tablespoons of soy sauce
- One tablespoon of hoisin sauce
- One teaspoon of sesame oil
- 2 teaspoons of water
- 100 milligrams of cornstarch
- As a garnish, use green onions

Directions:

1. Cook the sesame oil in a large skillet over medium-high heat until it is boiling.
2. It is recommended that the tofu be stirred on occasion until it reaches a golden brown color. To the skillet, add the garlic that has been minced as well as the tofu of cubes.
3. When the vegetables are done but still crisp, add a variety of them to the skillet and sauté them.
4. Take a small bowl and combine the hoisin sauce, cornstarch slurry, and soy sauce. Mix all of the ingredients together completely. After whisking the sauce into the tofu and vegetables, wait for it to thicken before proceeding with the recipe.
5. Green onions that have been neatly sliced should be used as a garnish right before serving.

Nutritional Information (per serving):

- Total: kCal: 240 Protein: 15g Fat: 10g Carbs: 25g

39. Eggplant Parmesan

- Twenty minutes for preparation
- Cooking Period: 40 Minutes
- Serves: 4.

Ingredients:

- One big eggplant cut into rounds
- one cup of breadcrumbs
- Grated Parmesan cheese, half a cup
- two beaten eggs
- Two cups of marinara sauce
- One cup of finely shredded mozzarella cheese
- For garnish, use fresh basil.

Directions:

1. Preheat the oven to 375 degrees Fahrenheit (190 degrees Celsius).
2. Coat the eggplant slices in a breadcrumb and Parmesan cheese mixture after dipping them in beaten eggs.
3. Once the eggplant slices have been coated, transfer them to a baking sheet that has been lined with parchment paper. Bake them for twenty-five to thirty minutes, or until they are completely cooked through and have a good brown color.
4. A layer of marinara sauce should be placed on a baking dish, and then baked eggplant slices should be arranged on top of the sauce.
5. On top, sprinkle the remaining marinara sauce and mozzarella cheese that has been shredded.

6. Continue baking for a further 15–20 minutes, after which the cheese should be bubbling and melted.
7. Sprinkle some fresh basil leaves on top before serving. serving.

Nutritional Information (per serving):

- Total: kCal: 320 Protein: 15g Fat: 15g Carbs: 30g

40. Chicken and Vegetable Skewers

- 15 minutes for preparation
- Cooking Period: 15 minutes
- Serves: Two

Ingredients:

- Two hen breasts, sliced into squares
- One bell pepper, chopped into pieces
- One sliced zucchini
- One red onion, sliced into pieces
- one-fourth cup olive oil
- two minced garlic cloves
- One teaspoon of dried oregano
- To taste, add salt and pepper.

Directions:

1. Bring the grill or grill pan up to a temperature that is somewhere between medium and hot.
2. Combine the olive oil, minced garlic, dried oregano, salt, and pepper in a bowl and whisk them together until they are thoroughly combined.
3. At the same time, skewer bell pepper chunks, zucchini slices, red onion chunks, and cubes of chicken.
4. A coating of the olive oil mixture should be applied to the skewers after they have been placed on the grill.

While stirring the mixture on a regular basis, continue cooking for ten to fifteen minutes, or until the chicken is fully cooked and the vegetables are soft.
5. Reheat the meal.

Nutritional Information (per serving):

- Total: kCal: 280 Protein: 25g Fat: 15g Carbs: 10g

41. Butternut Squash and Kale Salad

- 15 minutes for preparation
- Cooking Duration: 25 minutes
- Serves: Two

Ingredients:

- Two cups of butternut squash, diced
- four cups chopped kale
- 1/4 cup of cranberries, dried
- one-fourth cup of pumpkin seeds
- Two tablespoons of olive oil
- One tablespoon balsamic vinegar
- One tablespoon of maple syrup
- To taste, add salt and pepper.

Directions:

1. At a temperature of 400 degrees Fahrenheit, or 200 degrees Celsius, the oven should be set. Place the butternut squash cubes in a single layer on a baking sheet, season them with salt and pepper, and then spray them with olive oil before sending them into the oven. It should take between 25 and 30 minutes for the meat to be cooked through when it is roasted.

2. It is recommended that you place the kale in a big bowl and massage it with olive oil for a few minutes in order to soften it.
3. It is suggested that you top the bowl with roasted butternut squash, dried cranberries, and pumpkin seeds.
4. To prepare the dressing, take a separate bowl and combine the balsamic vinegar and maple syrup by whisking them together carefully. The salad should be tossed to mix all of the ingredients after the dressing has been added.
5. Serve immediately.

Nutritional Information (per serving):

- Total: kCal: 280 Protein: 7g Fat: 15g Carbs: 35g

42. Beef and Broccoli Stir-Fry

- 15 minutes for preparation
- Cooking Period: 15 minutes
- Serves: Two

Ingredients:

- Half a pound of finely cut beef sirloin
- two cups florets of broccoli
- One sliced bell pepper and two chopped garlic cloves
- Two tablespoons of soy sauce
- One tablespoon of oyster sauce
- One teaspoon of sesame oil
- One teaspoon cornstarch and two teaspoons water
- Sunflower seeds as a garnish

Directions:

1. Combine the soy sauce, sesame oil, oyster sauce, and cornstarch slurry in a bowl. Save at a later time.
2. Heat the oil in a big skillet over medium-high heat. Once the steak has browned, add the meat pieces and minced garlic to the sauce and stir.
3. Add the sliced bell pepper and the broccoli florets to the skillet after the vegetables are crisp-tender.
4. Pour the sauce mixture over the meat and vegetables, stirring constantly, until the sauce thickens.
5. Add some sesame seeds to the dish before serving.

Nutritional Information (per serving):

- Total: kCal: 320 Protein: 25g Fat: 15g Carbs: 20g

43. Mediterranean Chickpea Salad

- Prep Time: 10 min
- Cook Time: 0 min
- Serves: 4

Ingredients:

- Two cans of rinsed and drained chickpeas
- One diced cucumber
- one diced bell pepper
- one-fourth cup of finely chopped red onion
- 1/4 cup of crumbled feta cheese
- Slicing 1/4 cup of Kalamata olives
- Two tablespoons of olive oil
- One tablespoon of lemon juice
- One teaspoon of dried oregano
- Add salt and pepper to taste. Garnish with fresh parsley.

Directions:

1. In a large bowl, toss together the chickpeas, chopped cucumber, red onion, bell pepper, and crumbled feta cheese.
2. To make the dressing, fully mix the lemon juice, olive oil, dried oregano, salt, and pepper in a small basin.
3. Drizzle the chickpea mixture with the dressing, tossing to coat thoroughly.
4. Add some fresh parsley right before serving.

Nutritional Information (per serving):

- Total: kCal: 280 Protein: 12g Fat: 10g Carbs: 35g

44. Cauliflower Rice Stir-Fry

- Ten minutes for preparation
- Cooking Period: 15 minutes
- Serves: Two

Ingredients:

- 1 small head cauliflower, grated into rice-like pieces
- 1 cup mixed vegetables (such as peas, carrots, and corn)
- two beaten eggs
- two minced garlic cloves
- Two tablespoons of soy sauce
- One tablespoon of sesame oil
- One teaspoon of ginger, two grated green onions, and optionally chopped sesame seeds as a garnish

Directions:

1. Within a large skillet, bring the sesame oil to a temperature of medium. Grate the ginger and mince the garlic, then sauté the mixture for one minute.
2. Garlic and ginger should be moved to one side of the skillet, and eggs that have been beaten should be

poured onto the other side. The garlic and ginger should be mixed in after the scrambled eggs have been cooked thoroughly.
3. To the skillet, add a variety of veggies, and cook them until they are soft.
4. The cauliflower should be cooked for an additional five to seven minutes after the addition of the soy sauce and the rice made from cauliflower.
5. Immediately prior to serving, garnish with chopped green onions and toasted sesame seeds.

Nutritional Information (per serving):
- Total: kCal: 220 Protein: 12g Fat: 10g Carbs: 25g

45. Greek Yogurt Chicken Salad

- Prep Time: 10 min
- Cook Time: 15 min
- Serves: 2

Ingredients:

- Two cooked, shredded chicken breasts
- A quarter of a cup Greek yogurt
- 1/4 cup chopped cucumbers, 1/4 cup chopped bell pepper, 1/4 cup chopped red onion
- 1/4 cup of just-picked dill
- One tsp lemon juice
- Add salt and pepper to taste.
- Lettuce leaves for serving

Directions:

1. In a bowl, mix together the shredded chicken, Greek yogurt, sliced cucumber, diced bell pepper, diced red onion, chopped dill, lemon juice, salt, and pepper.

2. The mixture should be well-combined and creamy.
3. Salad leaves are used to serve the chicken salad.

Nutritional Information (per serving):

- Total: kCal: 280 Protein: 35g Fat: 7g Carbs: 15g

Snacks

46. Avocado and Tomato Salad

- Five minutes for preparation
- Cooking Period: None
- Serves: Two

Ingredients:

- 1 ripe avocado, diced
- Half a cup of cherry tomatoes
- A couple of tsp of extra virgin olive oil
- A solitary spoonful of balsamic vinegar
- To taste, add salt and pepper.

Directions:

1. Diced avocado and cherry tomatoes that have been cut in half should be mixed together in a bowl.
2. The olive oil and balsamic vinegar should be drizzled on top.
3. Add salt and pepper, then gently toss everything together to blend.

Serving Total:

kCal: 132 Protein: 2 g Fat: 12 g Carbs: 6 g

47. Greek Yogurt with Berries

- Two minutes for preparation
- Cooking Period: None
- Serves: One

Ingredients:

- half a cup of Greek yogurt
- 1/4 cup of mixed berries, including strawberries, raspberries, and blueberries
- One teaspoon honey, optional

Directions:

1. Greek yoghurt should be spooned into a serving bowl.
2. Add a variety of berries on top.
3. You can drizzle honey on top if you like.

Serving Total:

- kCal: 100 Protein: 10 g Fat: 0 g Carbs: 15 g

48. Cucumber Hummus Bites

- Ten minutes for preparation
- Cooking Period: None
- Serves: Two

Ingredients:

- 1 cucumber, sliced into rounds
- 1/2 cup hummus
- Paprika for garnish

Directions:

1. The rounds of cucumber should be placed on a serving plate.

2. Take a small amount of hummus and place it on top of each cucumber round.
3. To serve as a garnish, sprinkle with paprika.

Serving Total:

- kCal: 80 Protein: 4 g Fat: 3 g Carbs: 10 g

49. Almond Butter and Banana Rice Cakes

- Five minutes for preparation
- Cooking Period: None
- Serves: Two

Ingredients:

- Two cakes of rice
- Two tablespoons of almond butter
- One ripe banana, cut.

Directions:

1. Almond butter should be spread on rice cakes in an equal layer.
2. Put some sliced banana on top.
3. Serve as soon as possible.

Serving Total:

- kCal: 180 Protein: 4 g Fat: 8 g Carbs: 25 g

50. Caprese Skewers

- Ten minutes for preparation
- Cooking Period: None
- Serves: Two

Ingredients:

- Ten little tomatoes

- Ten little mozzarella sticks adorned with vibrant basil leaves
- Drizzle with balsamic glaze.

Directions:

1. A cherry tomato, a mozzarella ball, and a basil leaf should be skewered onto skewers simultaneously.
2. Repeat until all of the ingredients have been utilized.
3. Apply a glaze made with balsamic vinegar just before serving.

Serving Total:

- kCal: 120 Protein: 8 g Fat: 8 g Carbs: 5 g

51. Smoked Salmon and Cucumber Rolls

- Ten minutes for preparation
- Cooking Period: None
- Serves: Two

Ingredients:

- 4 slices smoked salmon
- 1 cucumber, peeled into ribbons
- 2 tbsp cream cheese
- Fresh dill for garnish

Directions:

1. The slices of smoked salmon should be laid out.
2. Each slice should have a very thin coating of cream cheese spread on it.
3. To finish off the cream cheese, arrange the cucumber ribbons on top.
4. You can secure the salmon pieces with toothpicks once you roll them up.
5. Fresh dill should be used as a garnish before serving.

Serving Total:
- kCal: 140 Protein: 14 g Fat: 8 g Carbs: 3 g

52. Egg Salad Lettuce Wraps
- Ten minutes for preparation
- Cooking Period: 10 minutes
- Serves: Two

Ingredients:
- four sliced hard-boiled eggs
- Two tablespoons of Greek yogurt
- One teaspoon mustard
- To taste, add salt and pepper.
- Four substantial lettuce leaves

Directions:
1. Eggs that have been diced, Greek yogurt, mustard, salt, and pepper should be combined in a bowl.
2. Egg salad should be spooned onto the lettuce leaves.
3. The lettuce leaves should be rolled up and served.

Serving Total:
- kCal: 180 Protein: 14 g Fat: 10 g Carbs: 5 g

53. Zucchini Chips
- Prep Time: 10 min
- Cooking Time: 25 min
- Serves: 2

Ingredients:
- Two medium zucchini, cut into thin slices
- Two tablespoons of olive oil
- 1/4 cup of Parmesan cheese, grated

- A half-tsp of garlic powder
- To taste, add salt and pepper.

Directions:

1. Preheat the oven to 375 degrees Fahrenheit (190 degrees Celsius).
2. In a bowl, mix the garlic powder, salt, pepper, olive oil, and Parmesan cheese. Stir after adding the zucchini chunks.
3. Place the slices on a baking pan in a single layer.
4. Bake until the crust is golden brown, 25 to 30 minutes.
5. Allow food to cool before serving.

Serving Total:

- kCal: 120 Protein: 5 g Fat: 10 g Carbs: 4 g

54. Tuna Stuffed Mini Bell Peppers

- Prep Time: 15 min
- Cooking Time: 0 min
- Serves: 2

Ingredients:

- Six little bell peppers, cut in half and seeded
- One can of drained tuna
- Two tablespoons of mayonnaise
- One tablespoon of lemon juice
- To taste, add salt and pepper.

Directions:

1. Put the tuna, mayonnaise, lemon juice, salt, and pepper into a bowl and mix them together.
2. When filling each bell pepper half, spoon the tuna mixture inside.
3. To be served cold.

Serving Total:

- kCal: 160 Protein: 18 g Fat: 8 g Carbs: 5 g

55. Cottage Cheese with Pineapple

- Prep Time: 5 min
- Cooking Time: 0 min
- Serves: 2

Ingredients:

- 1 cup cottage cheese
- 1/2 cup diced pineapple

Directions:

1. Two serving bowls should each contain a portion of cottage cheese.
2. Place pineapple cubes on top of each one.
3. Serve as soon as possible.

Serving Total:

- kCal: 180 Protein: 24 g Fat: 2 g Carbs: 18 g

56. Walnut and Apple Slices

- Prep Time: 5 min
- Cooking Time: 0 min
- Serves: 2

Ingredients:

- 1 apple, thinly sliced; 1/4 cup chopped walnuts; 2 tablespoons honey
- Half a teaspoon of cinnamon

Directions:

1. Apple slices should be arranged on a plate.

2. Apple slices should be topped with walnuts that have been chopped.
3. Honey should be drizzled over the top.
4. Add some cinnamon to the mixture.
5. Serve as soon as possible.

Serving Total:

- kCal: 180 Protein: 2 g Fat: 9 g Carbs: 27 g

57. Tofu and Vegetable Skewers

- 15 minutes for preparation
- Cooking Period: 10 minutes
- Serves: Two

Ingredients:

- 8 oz cubed firm tofu and 1 chopped bell pepper
- One sliced zucchini
- One-fourth cup soy sauce
- Two tablespoons of olive oil
- One tablespoon of maple syrup
- One teaspoon of garlic powder

Directions:

1. A grill or grill pan should be heated to a medium temperature.
2. In a bowl, prepare the mixture by whisking together the soy sauce, olive oil, maple syrup, and garlic powder.
3. Create skewers by threading cubes of tofu, chunks of bell pepper, and slices of zucchini onto them.
4. The marinade should be applied on the skewers.
5. It is recommended that skewers be grilled for eight to ten minutes, turning them occasionally, until the tofu

has a golden brown color and the vegetables have become tender.
6. Warm the dish.

Serving Total:

- kCal: 220 Protein: 14 g Fat: 14 g Carbs: 12 g

58. Quinoa Salad with Chickpeas

- 15 minutes for preparation
- 15 minutes for cooking
- Serves: Two

Ingredients:

- Half a cup of cooked quinoa
- Half a cup of rinsed and drained canned chickpeas
- half a cucumber, chopped
- half a bell pepper, chopped
- 2 tablespoons freshly chopped parsley
- Two tablespoons of lemon juice
- Two tablespoons of olive oil
- To taste, add salt and pepper.

Directions:

1. In a big bowl, combine cooked quinoa, cooked chickpeas, cucumber, bell pepper, and parsley.
2. Whisk together the lemon juice, olive oil, salt, and pepper in a small bowl.
3. Drizzle the dressing over the quinoa mixture and then toss.
4. Serve cold or at room temperature.

Serving Total:

- kCal: 240 Protein: 8 g Fat: 10 g Carbs: 32 g

59. Roasted Chickpeas

- Prep Time: 5 min
- Cooking Time: 25 min
- Serves: 2

Ingredients:

- One can of washed and drained chickpeas
- One tablespoon of olive oil
- One teaspoon of paprika
- A half-tsp of garlic powder
- Add salt to taste.

Directions:

1. Set the oven's temperature to 200 degrees Celsius, or 400 degrees F.
2. Add the chickpeas, olive oil, paprika, garlic powder, and salt to a bowl and toss again.
3. Arrange the chickpeas on a baking sheet in a single layer.
4. Roast until the top is crisp, 20 to 25 minutes, stirring halfway through.
5. Before serving, let the food cool.

Serving Total:

- kCal: 160 Protein: 6 g Fat: 6 g Carbs: 20 g

60. Chocolate Covered Strawberries

- Prep Time: 10 min
- Cooking Time: 5 min
- Serves: 2

Ingredients:

- 1 cup strawberries

- 2 oz dark chocolate, melted

Directions:

1. Place parchment paper on a baking pan and set it aside.
2. Each strawberry should be coated halfway with molten dark chocolate before being dipped.
3. Place on the baking sheet that has been prepared.
4. Chill for ten to fifteen minutes, or until the chocolate has hardened.
5. To be served cold.

Serving Total:

- kCal: 120 Protein: 2 g Fat: 8 g Carbs: 15 g

Hydration and Beverages

61. Lemon Cucumber Mint Infused Water

- Prep Time: 5 min
- Cook Time: 0 min
- Serves: 4

Ingredients:

- One cucumber
- one lemon
- ten fresh mint leaves
- four cups of water

Directions:

1. It is recommended to place lemon slices, cucumber slices, and mint leaves in a pitcher.

2. The ingredients should be poured with water.
3. Ensure that the dish is chilled for at least one hour before serving.

Nutritional Information: (Per Serving)

- Calories: 5
- Protein: 0g
- Fat: 0g
- Carbs: 2g

62. Pineapple Ginger Green Tea

- Prep Time: 5 min
- Cook Time: 5 min
- Serves: 2

Ingredients:

- 2 cups water
- 2 green tea bags
- 1 cup pineapple chunks
- 1-inch piece of ginger, sliced

Directions:

1. After bringing a pot of water to a boil, turn off the heat.
2. For three to five minutes, steep green tea bags in hot water.
3. Before serving, remove the tea bags and let the tea come to room temperature.
4. Puree the pineapple chunks and ginger in a blender until very smooth.
5. Green tea ought to be incorporated with the mixture.
6. Place on top of ice chips.

Nutritional Information: (Per Serving)

- Calories: 45

- Protein: 0g
- Fat: 0g
- Carbs: 12g

63. Watermelon Lime Electrolyte Drink

- Five minutes for preparation
- Cooking Period: 0 minutes
- Serves: Two

Ingredients:

- 2 cups watermelon, cubed
- Juice of 2 limes
- 1/4 tsp sea salt
- 2 cups coconut water

Directions:

1. Puree the watermelon cubes and lime juice in a blender until the mixture is completely smooth.
2. If pulp is desired, the mixture can be strained to eliminate it.
3. Toss in the coconut water and the sea salt first.
4. To be served cold.

Nutritional Information: (Per Serving)

- Calories: 60
- Protein: 1g
- Fat: 0g
- Carbs: 15g

64. Berry Blast Hydration Smoothie

- Five minutes for preparation.
- Cooking Time: Not at all
- Serves two

Ingredients:

- One cup of mixed berries, including raspberries, blueberries, and strawberries
- half a cup of Greek yogurt, plain
- half a cup of almond milk
- One tablespoon of honey

Directions:

1. In a blender, combine all the ingredients.
2. Blend until the mixture is very smooth.
3. Transfer the blend into glasses and promptly serve.

Nutritional Information: (Per Serving)

- Calories: 90
- Protein: 6g
- Fat: 2g
- Carbs: 15g

65. Citrus Mint Cooler

- Prep Time: 5 min
- Cook Time: 0 min
- Serves: 2

Ingredients:

- 2 oranges, peeled and segmented
- 1 lemon, peeled and sliced
- 1 lime, peeled and sliced
- 10 fresh mint leaves
- 2 cups sparkling
- water

Directions:

1. To prepare the mint leaves, gently muddle them in a pitcher.
2. Orange segments, lemon slices, and lime slices should be added to the mixture.
3. The mixture should be overflowed with sparkling water.
4. In order to mix, gently stir.
5. Serve atop ice chips.

Nutritional Information: (Per Serving)

- Calories: 25
- Protein: 1g
- Fat: 0g
- Carbs: 6g

66. Cucumber Basil Detox Water

- Prep Time: 5 min
- Cook Time: 0 min
- Serves: 4

Ingredients:

- 1 cucumber, sliced
- 10 fresh basil leaves
- 4 cups water
- Ice cubes
-

Directions:

1. The cucumber slices and basil leaves should be mixed together in a pitcher.
2. The pitcher should be filled with water.
3. In order to infuse the flavors, refrigerate the mixture for half an hour.

4. Serve atop ice chips.

Nutritional Information: (Per Serving)

- Calories: 0
- Protein: 0g
- Fat: 0g
- Carbs: 0g

67. Mango Coconut Water Refresher

- Prep Time: 5 min
- Cook Time: 0 min
- Serves: 2

Ingredients:

- 1 ripe mango, peeled and diced
- 2 cups coconut water
- 1/2 lime, juiced
- Ice cubes

Directions:

1. Blend the mango in a blender until it is completely smooth.
2. Put the mango puree, coconut water, and lime juice into a pitcher and mix them together.
3. To blend, give it a thorough stir.
4. Serve atop ice chips.

Nutritional Information: (Per Serving)

- Calories: 80
- Protein: 1g
- Fat: 0g
- Carbs: 20g

68. Raspberry Rosemary Infused Water

- Prep Time: 5 min
- Cook Time: 0 min
- Serves: 4

Ingredients:

- 1 cup fresh raspberries
- 2 sprigs fresh rosemary
- 4 cups water
- Ice cubes

Directions:

1. Mix the rosemary and raspberries together in a pitcher using a gentle muddle.
2. The pitcher should be filled with water.
3. Keep in the refrigerator for at least one hour.
4. Serve atop ice chips.

Nutritional Information: (Per Serving)

- Calories: 10
- Protein: 0g
- Fat: 0g
- Carbs: 2g

69. Turmeric Ginger Lemonade

- Prep Time: 10 min
- Cook Time: 0 min
- Serves: 2

Ingredients:

- 2 cups water
- 2 tbsp honey
- 1-inch piece of fresh ginger, grated
- 1/2 tsp ground turmeric
- Juice of 2 lemons

- Ice cubes

Directions:

1. The water should be heated in a small saucepan over a low heat.
2. Honey, grated ginger, and ground turmeric should be stirred in until the honey is completely dissolved.
3. Take it off the stove and let it to cool down.
4. Add the lemon juice after it has cooled down.
5. Serve atop ice chips.

Nutritional Information: (Per Serving)

- Calories: 50
- Protein: 0g
- Fat: 0g
- Carbs: 13g

70. Blueberry Basil Smash

- Prep Time: 5 min
- Cook Time: 0 min
- Serves: 2

Ingredients:

- 1 cup fresh blueberries
- 10 fresh basil leaves
- 2 cups water
- Ice cubes

Directions:

1. In a pitcher, combine the basil leaves and blueberries and muddle them gently.
2. Pour some water into the pitcher.
3. Store in the fridge for a minimum of sixty minutes.
4. Place on top of ice chips.

Nutritional Information: (Per Serving)

- Calories: 15
- Protein: 0g
- Fat: 0g
- Carbs: 4g

71. Peach Lavender Iced Tea

- Prep Time: 5 min
- Cook Time: 5 min
- Serves: 2

Ingredients:

- 2 cups water
- 2 black tea bags
- 1 ripe peach, sliced
- 1 tbsp dried lavender
- Ice cubes

Directions:

1. A pot should be used to bring water to a boil.
2. Tea bags and dried lavender should be added once the heat has been removed.
3. Allow to steep for a period of five minutes.
4. Tea bags and lavender should be removed.
5. Wait until the tea has reached room temperature before placing it in the refrigerator to chill.
6. Slices of peach should be served on top of ice.

Nutritional Information: (Per Serving)

- Calories: 10
- Protein: 0g
- Fat: 0g

- Carbs: 3g

72. Apple Cinnamon Spice Infused Water

- Prep Time: 5 min
- Cook Time: 0 min
- Serves: 4

Ingredients:

- 1 apple, thinly sliced
- 2 cinnamon sticks
- 4 cups water
- Ice cubes

Directions:

1. The apple slices and cinnamon sticks should be mixed together in a pitcher.
2. The pitcher should be filled with water.
3. Keep in the refrigerator for at least one hour.
4. Serve atop ice chips.

Nutritional Information: (Per Serving)

- Calories: 10
- Protein: 0g
- Fat: 0g
- Carbs: 3g

73. Pomegranate Mint Spritzer

- Prep Time: 5 min
- Cook Time: 0 min
- Serves: 2

Ingredients:

- 1/2 cup pomegranate seeds
- 10 fresh mint leaves

- 2 cups sparkling water
- Ice cubes

Directions:

1. Combine the pomegranate seeds and mint leaves in a glass and gently muddle them together.
2. The glass should be filled with carbonated water.
3. In order to mix, gently stir.
4. Serve atop ice chips.

Nutritional Information: (Per Serving)

- Calories: 20
- Protein: 0g
- Fat: 0g
- Carbs: 5g

74. Watermelon Basil Cooler

- Prep Time: 5 min
- Cook Time: 0 min
- Serves: 2

Ingredients:

- 2 cups watermelon, cubed
- 10 fresh basil leaves
- 2 cups coconut water
- Ice cubes

Directions:

1. Blend watermelon until it is completely smooth in a blender.
2. To prepare the basil leaves, gently muddle them in a pitcher.
3. The watermelon puree and the coconut water should be poured into the mixing container.

4. To blend, give it a thorough stir.
   5. Serve atop ice chips.

Nutritional Information: (Per Serving)

- Calories: 70
- Protein: 1g
- Fat: 0g
- Carbs: 17g

75. Kiwi Mint Refresher

- Prep Time: 5 min
- Cook Time: 0 min
- Serves: 2

Ingredients:

- 2 kiwis, peeled and sliced
- 10 fresh mint leaves
- 2 cups water
- Ice cubes

Directions:

1. Put the mint leaves and kiwi slices in a pitcher and stir to combine.
2. Pour some water into the pitcher.
3. Store in the fridge for a minimum of sixty minutes.
4. Place on top of ice chips.

Nutritional Information: (Per Serving)

- Calories: 45
- Protein: 1g
- Fat: 0g
- Carbs: 11g

Dessert:

76. Avocado Chocolate Mousse

- Prep Time: 10 min
- Cook Time: 0 min
- Serves: 2

Ingredients:

- One mature avocado
- Two tablespoons of cocoa powder
- 2 tbsp honey or maple syrup
- Half a teaspoon of vanilla extract
- pinch of salt

Directions:

1. Begin by removing the flesh from the avocado and placing it in a blender.
2. Incorporate vanilla essence, honey or maple syrup, cocoa powder, and salt into the mixture.
3. Puree till it is silky smooth and creamy.

Nutritional Information:

- Total: kCal: 250 Protein: 4g Fat: 15g Carbs: 2g

77. Greek Yogurt Parfait

- Five minutes for preparation
- Cooking Period: 0 minutes
- Serves: One

Ingredients:

- 1/2 cup Greek yogurt
- 1/4 cup mixed berries (blueberries, raspberries, strawberries)

- 1 tbsp honey
- 1 tbsp chopped nuts (almonds, walnuts)

Directions:

1. Using a glass that is designed for serving, create a layer of Greek yogurt, mixed berries, honey, and chopped almonds with the intention of serving.
2. Once the glass is entirely full, continue to stack the layers until you reach the top.

Nutritional Information:

- Total: kCal: 210 Protein: 15g Fat: 8g Carbs: 25g

78. Banana Nice Cream

- Five minutes for preparation
- Cooking Period: 0 minutes
- Serves: Two

Ingredients:

- 2 ripe bananas, cut and frozen
- one-fourth cup almond milk
- One teaspoon vanilla extract

Directions:

1. In a blender, combine frozen banana slices, almond milk, and vanilla extract. Blend until smooth.
2. Puree till it is silky smooth and creamy.
3. If you want a more firm texture, you can freeze it or serve it immediately as soft-serve.

Nutritional Information:

- Total: kCal: 120 Protein: 2g Fat: 1g Carbs: 30g

79. Chia Seed Pudding

- **Prep Time:** 5 min + chilling
- **Cook Time:** 0 min
- **Serves:** 2

Ingredients:

- One-fourth cup chia seeds
- 1 cup almond milk without sugar
- 1 tablespoon maple syrup or honey
- Half a teaspoon vanilla extract
- Fresh fruit, such as kiwis or berries, to garnish

Directions:

1. In a dish, whisk together chia seeds, almond milk, honey (or maple syrup), and vanilla extract.
2. Refrigerate the mixture for at least two hours or overnight, stirring regularly until it thickens.
3. Store in the refrigerator and garnish with fresh fruit.

Nutritional Information:

- Total: kCal: 140 Protein: 5g Fat: 7g Carbs: 15g

80. Apple Slices with Almond Butter

- Five minutes for preparation
- Cooking Period: 0 minutes
- Serves: Two

Ingredients:

- 1 apple, sliced
- 2 tbsp almond butter
- Cinnamon (optional)

Directions:

1. Apple slices should be arranged on a plate.

2. Almond butter should be spread on each section of apple.
3. The cinnamon can be sprinkled on top if desired.

Nutritional Information:

- Total: kCal: 180 Protein: 4g Fat: 10g Carbs: 20g

81. Coconut Yogurt with Mixed Berries

- Five minutes for preparation
- Cooking Period: 0 minutes
- Serves: One

Ingredients:

- 1/2 cup coconut yogurt
- 1/4 cup mixed berries (blueberries, raspberries, strawberries)
- 1 tablespoon of coconut shreds
- One teaspoon of optional maple syrup or honey

Directions:

1. Coconut yogurt should be added to a bowl.
2. On top, sprinkle some shredded coconut and mixed berries, and if you choose, drizzle some honey or maple syrup over the yogurt.

Nutritional Information:

- Total: kCal: 150 Protein: 2g Fat: 8g Carbs: 18g

82. Chocolate Covered Strawberries

- Prep Time: 10 min
- Cook Time: 0 min
- Serves: 2

Ingredients:

- 10 strawberries, cleaned and dried
- 1/4 cup dark chocolate chips
- One teaspoon of coconut oil

Directions:

1. Melt the dark chocolate chips and coconut oil in a bowl that is safe for the microwave at intervals of thirty seconds until the mixture is smooth.
2. Each strawberry should be coated halfway with the molten chocolate before being dipped.
3. Place on a pan that has been lined with parchment paper, and place in the refrigerator until the chocolate has hardened.

Nutritional Information:

- Total: kCal: 120 Protein: 2g Fat: 7g Carbs: 15g

83. Mango Coconut Chia Pudding

- Five minutes plus cooling
- Cooking Period: 0 minutes
- Serves: Two

Ingredients:

- 1 chopped ripe mango and 1/4 cup of chia seeds
- One cup coconut milk
- 1 tablespoon maple syrup or honey

Directions:

1. Half of the diced mango should be pureed in a blender until it is completely done.
2. Chia seeds, coconut milk, pureed mango, and either honey or maple syrup should be in a bowl and mixed together.

3. Place in the refrigerator for at least two hours, or until the mixture has solidified.
4. The remaining diced mango should be sprinkled on top before serving cold.

Nutritional Information:

- Total: kCal: 220 Protein: 5g Fat: 15g Carbs: 20g

84. Nutty Date Balls

- Ten minutes for preparation
- Cooking Period: 0 minutes
- Serves: Eight

Ingredients:

- one cup of pitted dates
- 1/2 cup almonds
- 1/4 cup of coconut, shredded
- One tablespoon of cocoa powder
- One teaspoon vanilla extract

Directions:

1. Place the dates, almonds, shredded coconut, cocoa powder, and vanilla essence into a food processor and process until mixed together.
2. The mixture should be pulsed until it results in a sticky dough.
3. The ingredients should be rolled into little balls.
4. The balls can be rolled with cocoa powder or shredded coconut, but this step is optional.
5. Before serving, place in the refrigerator for half an hour.

Nutritional Information:

- Total: kCal: 100 Protein: 2g Fat: 5g Carbs: 15g

85. Grilled Pineapple with Cinnamon

- Five minutes for preparation
- Cooking Period: 5 minutes
- Serves: Two

Ingredients:

- Half a pineapple, cut into slices and peel
- One teaspoon of coconut oil
- One teaspoon of cinnamon

Directions:

1. Prepare a grill pan by heating it over medium heat and covering it with a thin layer of coconut oil.
2. To achieve a caramelized appearance, grill pineapple slices for two to three minutes on each side.
3. Immediately prior to serving, sprinkle with cinnamon.

Nutritional Information:

- Total: kCal: 90 Protein: 1g Fat: 3g Carbs: 20g

86. Raspberry Coconut Chia Popsicles

- Wait time: five minutes plus freezing
- Time to Cook: 0 minutes
- Serves four people

Ingredients:

- One cup of raspberries
- half a cup of coconut milk
- Two tablespoons of chia seeds
- 1 tablespoon maple syrup or honey

Directions:

1. The raspberries, coconut milk, and honey or maple syrup should be pureed in a blender until they are completely smooth.
2. Place the chia seeds in a bowl and let them sit for ten minutes.
3. After the liquid has been poured into the popsicle molds, insert the sticks.
4. At least four hours, or until the mixture is solid, freeze it.

Nutritional Information:

- Total: kCal: 70 Protein: 2g Fat: 4g Carbs: 8g

87. Almond Flour Cookies

- Ten minutes for preparation
- Cooking Period: 12 minutes
- Serves: Eight

Ingredients:

- one cup of flour made from almonds
- 1/4 cup of melted coconut oil
- 1/4 cup honey or maple syrup
- Salt and one tsp of vanilla extract

Directions:

1. Before you begin, make sure that the oven is preheated to 175 degrees Celsius (350 degrees Fahrenheit), and that a baking sheet has been completely lined with parchment paper.
2. In order to make a dough, you need put almond flour, melted coconut oil, honey or maple syrup, vanilla extract, and salt into a bowl and mix them together. Combine everything until it is completely smooth.

3. Create balls out of bits of dough by rolling them into a size that is comparable to that of a tablespoon. Once you have transferred them, place them on the baking sheet. Use a fork to distribute them in an equitable manner.
4. A total of ten to twelve minutes should be spent in the oven, or until the edges have a golden brown color.
5. Please allow it to cool before serving.

Nutritional Information:

- Total: kCal: 120 Protein: 2g Fat: 10g Carbs: 7g

88. Lemon Blueberry Frozen Yogurt

- Prepare in 5 minutes plus freeze
- Cooking Period: 0 minutes
- Serves: Two

Ingredients:

- One cup of Greek yogurt
- One lemon's zest and juice, half a cup of blueberries
- two tablespoons maple syrup or honey

Directions:

1. Greek yogurt, blueberries, lemon zest, lemon juice, and honey or maple syrup should be blended together in a blender prior to serving. Blend until it is completely smooth.
2. To ensure that no ice crystals form, transfer the mixture to a shallow dish and freeze it for three to four hours, stirring it every hour.
3. Spoon the frozen mixture into serving dishes and proceed with serving.

Nutritional Information:

- Total: kCal: 150 Protein: 10g Fat: 2g Carbs: 20g

89. Peanut Butter Banana Bites

- Prep Time: 5 min
- Cook Time: 0 min
- Serves: 2

Ingredients:

- 1 banana, sliced
- 2 tbsp peanut butter
- 2 tbsp granola

Directions:

1. The banana slices should be spread with peanut butter.
2. Grass the top with some granola.
3. Serve as soon as possible.

Nutritional Information:

- Total: kCal: 180 Protein: 5g Fat: 10g Carbs: 20g

90. Watermelon Mint Salad

- Ten minutes for preparation
- Cooking Period: 0 minutes
- Serves: 4.

Ingredients:

- four cups watermelon sliced
- 1/4 cup freshly cut mint leaves and 1 lime's juice
- One tablespoon maple syrup or honey (optional)

Directions:

1. Combine watermelon that has been diced and mint leaves that have been cut in a big basin.
2. The salad should be tossed with lime juice after it has been squeezed over it.

3. Depending on your preference, drizzle with honey or maple syrup.
4. To be served cold.

Nutritional Information:

- Total: kCal: 60 Protein: 1g Fat: 0g Carbs: 15g

FREE SUPPLEMENTARY STUDY RESOURCES

√ 65 Flash Cards with additional special recipes for your intermittent fasting.

√ 28-Day Food Plan printable board to hang in your kitchen

If you enjoyed our book, please give us a spontaneous review and scan the Qr Code: it will only take a minute of your time, but it is very important to us. Many thanks.

SCAN THE QRCODE TO DOWNLOAD THE FREE BONUSES

OTHERWISE TYPE IN THIS ADDRESS:

https://bit.ly/3Q1U2yo

Improve your awareness of how to burn superfluous fat and lose weight by boosting your energy and regulating your metabolism with our exclusive free bonus, included in the book "INTERMITTENT FASTING FOR SMART WOMEN OVER 50."

Expand your results with our free downloadable resources by experts. These tools, designed to enhance your knowledge and refine your approach to intermittent fasting, are the key to unlocking the next level of success.

Made in the USA
Middletown, DE
23 March 2025